A Black Future?

RONALD NICOLSON

A Black Future?

Jesus and Salvation in South Africa

SCM PRESS

London

TRINITY PRESS INTERNATIONAL

Philadelphia

First published 1990

SCM Press Ltd
26–30 Tottenham Road
London N1 4BZ

Trinity Press International
3725 Chestnut Street
Philadelphia, Pa. 19104

British Library Cataloguing in Publication Data

Nicolson, Ronald
    A black future?: Jesus and salvation in South Africa.
    1. South Africa. Christian theology
    I. Title
    230'.0968

ISBN 0–334–00120–X

Library of Congress Cataloging-in-Publication Data

Nicolson, Ronald
    A Black future? Jesus and salvation in South Africa / Ronald
Nicolson.
        p.   cm.
    Includes bibliographical references.
    ISBN 0–334–00120–X
    1. Christianity—South Africa.   2. Jesus Christ—Person and
offices.   3. Salvation.   4. South Africa—History—Philosophy.
5. Race relations—Religious aspects—Christianity.   6. South
Africa—Race relations.   7. Black theology.   8. Liberation theology.
9. South Africa—Church history—20th century.   I. Title.
BR1450.N53   1990   89–28180
276.8'0828—dc20

Typeset at The Spartan Press Ltd, Lymington, Hants
and printed in Great Britain by
Billing and Sons Ltd, Worcester .

Contents

For Lindiwe

Preface

Most of this book was written during a year's sabbatical leave from my teaching responsibilities, for which, and for their financial support, I am very grateful to the University of Natal.

The financial assistance of the Institute for Research Development of the Human Sciences Research Council towards this research is also hereby acknowledged. Opinions expressed in this book and conclusions arrived at are those of the author and do not necessarily represent the views of the Institute for Research Development or the Human Sciences Research Council.

I was privileged to spend much of my sabbatical time as an Honorary Research Fellow at King's College, London, and would like to express my warm thanks to Stuart Hall, who made it all possible, and also to Colin Gunton, Christoph Schwöbel and others there who welcomed me and permitted me to pick their brains in discussions and seminars. They will not necessarily agree with very much in this book, but I gained a great deal from listening to them, and the book is more balanced than it would otherwise have been.

I also spent a semester at Union Seminary, New York. My indebtedness to Tom Driver and the 'ST271' class will, I hope, be obvious. Less obvious but also greatly appreciated was the benefit of working in the elegant, comfortable and well-stocked library at Union. I am grateful, too, to Dean Fenhagen for making it possible to use the library resources at General Theological Seminary.

My stay at Union would have been impossible without the warm and loving hospitality extended by Hays Rockwell and the congregation at St James's Church, Madison Avenue, New York. Whatever small value this book may have to others, the value to me, who have benefitted from all these friendships, is incalculable.

I was greatly helped by research work done by the Revd Solomon Jacob which pointed me in the direction of much useful material.

My wife Gail read through the entire typescript several times to correct my grammar and to force me to write in comprehensible English. I thank her for this labour of love.

Introduction

This book is an attempt to build some sort of bridge between the theology of Europe and America and the theology of the Third World. The two seem to have little in common. They are aimed at different audiences, and answer different questions. Yet it may be that each has something to learn from the other. Certainly it is not right that First-World theology should continue to ignore the very different and perhaps more urgent theological issues faced in poor Third-World countries, and in so far as it does so it deserves all the scorn that Third-World theology sometimes directs towards it. But Third-World liberation theology, and more specifically Black South African theology, engaged as it is in the heat of the struggle, needs, I believe, the intellectual underpinning that First-World theology can provide if its answers are to be credible.

In the 1970s English theology was very concerned about christology. The fierce debate centring upon *The Myth of God Incarnate*[1] seems to have fizzled out, or to have moved on to even more controversial ground. The question now is not so much 'Is Jesus God?', but 'Does God as a personal entity exist?' The theological enterprise involves balancing up the fruits of biblical scholarship, the questions raised by 'cultured despisers' and the need to preserve some significance for Christian belief and identity in a modern secular world.

Third-World theology in its different forms – liberation, Black, Minjung, etc. – is also concerned with christology and with the existence of God. Unlike English theology it is not really interested in questions like 'Is Jesus God?' or 'Does God exist?' It assumes the truth of a divine-human Jesus, and of the presence of a loving God, and asks how that faith can be harnessed to help with the struggle to throw off the chains of colonial and capitalist exploitation. Many

Third-World theologians would regard the concerns of First-World theology as irrelevant and time-wasting.

Another book about christology seems *passé*; another book about contextual theology unnecessary in an already flooded market. The publication of *The Myth of God Incarnate* brought into the public eye issues which go back at least to the period of the Enlightenment and the Deists, perhaps back to the days before the Nicene Creed and the Chalcedonian Definition of orthodox Christian belief about who Jesus was. Can there be anything new to say?

My concern in this book, however, is not only 'Is traditional Christian belief about Jesus true?', but 'Is it helpful, does it make any effective difference?' Jesus, however he is understood, has been the pivot of Christian faith because people have believed that he made God real for them and available to them. He is seen to be the means through which God deals with the world. Believing in a god or gods who exist in some academic sense on some inaccessible Olympia, far from human concerns except for occasional forays into the created world, is not the same as believing in a God who is intimately, constantly, purposefully, transformingly, part of our being and existence. Christians believe that Jesus makes this kind of difference to our relationship with God. To put it crudely and provocatively, they believe that Jesus makes God 'useful' to us.

Of course from a theological point of view that last sentence is very wrong. 'The chief end of man is to glorify God', said the Westminster Shorter Catechism; not 'the chief end of God is to be useful to human beings'.[2] Of course (if there is a God) it has to be true that God is primary, that we are totally dependent on him, if God is what we mean by God. Nevertheless, if God is to be God, he must be the pivot or the foundation – or whatever other metaphor we may choose to use to indicate that it is God who gives life – who gives meaning to existence. He is not an irrelevant God, and if he were, our meaning of the word 'God' would have changed. Even the call to worship God is a call made for our sake. God does not need our worship – or he is not God. We need to worship him, to give meaning and centre to our lives.

Whatever meaning may in theory be ascribed to the word 'G-O-D', Christian belief is surely that the God of our faith does not remain isolated or irrelevant or an occasional *deus ex machina*, a sort of once-off bolt from the blue, but makes himself constantly available to us. He helps us. He saves us. It is also basic Christian belief that it is through Jesus that this availability of God is especially channelled. If all this is not true, then there is no point in

Christian faith. Jesus is the one who manifests and mediates the love and gracious help of God to us.

So it seems to me worthwhile to return to the christological debate, but from a somewhat different perspective from the form which some of the debate thus far has taken. In a post-Enlightenment Western world, there has been a concern to make Christian belief acceptable to a community which no longer accepts truth on other people's authority but wants personal and empirical evidence of that truth. We can, of course, argue about whether post-Enlightenment empiricists are really as independent from external authority as they think they are, and we will indeed touch on this argument later.[3] For the moment my point is only that, whether rightly or wrongly, post-Enlightenment Western philosophers, after centuries of authoritative church dogmatism culminating in the blood of the Reformation, have largely insisted that concepts must make logical sense, must be reasonable, must be consistent with empirical experience. Philosophers like Hume and Kant have been very influential in England. Much of the christological debate has been concerned with whether traditional belief in Jesus as being divine as well as human is in fact a rational, reasonable belief, and revisionary ideas about Jesus have been shaped in order to meet the rationalist challenge.

Section I of the book is an attempt to summarize some of the issues that have been raised in the christological debate to date. I will suggest that there are indeed quite serious historical and logical problems in traditional belief about Jesus. On the other hand I will suggest that because we know very little, if anything, of what it could mean to be God, and not even very much about what it means to be human, we cannot become modern dogmatists and rule out *a priori* the idea that Jesus is both divine and human. Is that perhaps why at present the debate has fizzled out? Perhaps there is no more to be said on either side. The logical problems are apparent, but the traditional rejoinders are equally weighty, given the mystery about divine and human nature, thus bringing the debate to a point of stalemate.

But since the belief in Jesus as being both divine and human arose as a logical entailment of belief in Jesus as Saviour, perhaps this is another starting point to the debate. Jon Sobrino[4] suggests that the post-Enlightenment challenge to traditional christological doctrine consisted not only in the logical challenge from Hume but also in the practical challenge of Marx. Faith in Jesus has to be shown to be effective in liberation. Does Jesus, or faith in Jesus, liberate people from their bondage? If so, how? We need to try to understand not only how Jesus was perceived as saviour through New Testament eyes and the eyes of subsequent tradition, but how he can be perceived as saviour in our own circumstances. Jesus was born to a particular place and people with their particular problems. Yet Christian faith believes him to be of universal significance to all places, times and people. We will have to see whether, and how, that is true.

Edward Schillebeeckx says that the crisis for modern Christians

> . . . lies in the fact that Jesus is still regularly explained to us as salvation and grace in terms which are no longer valid for our world of experience, i.e. in terms of earlier experiences; and on the other hand in the fact that we seem no longer capable in words or actions to 'make a defence for the hope that is in us'.[5]

Section II of the book examines some of the ways in which Jesus has been perceived as saviour in the past, and asks: does this perception still fit our own experience? We cannot ignore the tradition. Our present circumstances and our present faith grow out of the past. There are universal truths and universal human experiences which overarch the ages.

> Present and past are not 'two things' in juxtaposition. In reality, the message of the New Testament and our present experiences do not stand over against each other and alongside each other as two things. They already touch each other.[6]

Nevertheless we need to ask ourselves just what, in the common experience of past and present, is still real for us, and what constitutes a universal truth about the saving work of Jesus to which we can still say 'Amen'. To quote Schillebeeckx yet again,

> Christians who continue to experience decisive faith in Jesus will be able to invite others to renewed possibilities of experience, if they search from their own Christian self understanding for something in our present pattern of experience of salvation from God in Jesus.[7]

and,

> in my view this gulf between *faith* [Schillebeeckx means here the faith received from our fathers, the faith of the church] and *experience* is one of the fundamental reasons for the present day crisis among Christians who are faithful to the church.[8]

I wish to ask, then, whether the received understandings of faith are still true to our experience. And since 'our' is a widely encompassing word, I narrow it down to my own time and place, and to understandings of salvation for an oppressed people. I live and work in South Africa. I try to ask how salvation can work in the South African situation.

In section III of the book I look at theologies which claim to be theologies of the oppressed. I look at Latin American liberation theology, and at what can be learned from the still very new and yet-to-be-developed field of Black theology. I try to understand from the outside what these theologians are saying. It is true that I am neither oppressed (relatively speaking: none of us is ever entirely free of political and economic restraints) nor black. Yet until black people are free, I cannot be free. Their concerns are, or should be, my concerns. I make no attempt here to tell those who are oppressed how they should think, or to impose my own interpretations upon them. The reflections are purely my own as I try to discover how I can best interpret Jesus within the tragic circumstances of my own country.

To indulge in speculative theology while an intense struggle is raging, a struggle in which at present I do not bear more than a tiny part of the suffering that ordinary black families endure, may seem heartless and frivolous. The concerns of Third-World theology are of great importance to the concerns of Western theology outlined in section I. Third-World theology attempts to show just how it is that Jesus is relevant to the situation of the Third World, how he saves, what he does. Whether their answers are right is another matter: but their questions are the ones that First-World theology needs to be asking as well.

Yet the philosophical concerns of Western theology are surely not irrelevant to Third-World theology, either. Unless we can show that belief in Jesus as saviour is a reasonable belief, then he is not a saviour but a false crutch, a superstition which may comfort but has no solid basis in reality.

Thus in section IV I attempt to construct an understanding of Jesus and a model of salvation in Jesus which takes both experience and logic into account. I offer my reflections in the belief that philosophical and theological attempts to understand, to discover meaning, are an important part of any movement of social change, and as a humble contribution to that cause. In the South African agony, or all other agonies that surround us in our world, can Jesus still save us? How? Who is he for us? What must we do to be saved?

I do think these questions are relevant. Most South Africans, black and white, are Christian, or claim to be. If Jesus can save, then there is, after all, hope for the 'Beloved Country'.[9] To understand that hope might change the course of events. If we can find no meaning in or content to the notion of salvation in Jesus, then we must put our hope elsewhere, or surrender all hope and let the tragedy take its inevitable course. The answers, however speculative, however academic, however removed from the front line of battle, do matter.

In order to give real context to the questions which I ask, I have chosen to ask them with a real person in mind. Sipho Mkhize figures quite prominently in sections II and III. He is a real person, although Sipho is not his real name. The facts about him and his family are true, and fairly typical for many black people in South Africa today. Yet my thoughts, of course, are mine and not Sipho's. It is possible that Sipho would view the questions and the answers quite differently. I cannot think his thoughts. But in South Africa I cannot think theologically without having Sipho and others like him constantly in mind. Because of the structure of my argument, we do not actually meet Sipho until Chapter 2 of the second section; readers impatient with the theological discussions of the first section may want to turn to that chapter first, but they will understand the exploration of the burning problem it raises better if they have also read the first section.

I

Jesus
Human and Divine

1

The New Testament

If we are to talk about Jesus at all, our first question must surely be, what does the New Testament say? How did Jesus describe himself? How did the first Christians perceive him? The Chalcedonian fathers, says Bray,[1] certainly saw themselves as making explicit what was always implicit in the New Testament. For many Christians, this is the end of the argument. The New Testament teaches that Jesus was fully divine and fully human, therefore this definition cannot be doubted, and all that remains is perhaps to explore any further implications of this for faith. Thus Michael Green, referring to C. F. D. Moule's *The Origin of Christology*,[2] can say that 'it is probable that if his book had been available a year ago *The Myth of God Incarnate* would not have seen the light of day'.[3] Since Moule's book, at least in Green's view, shows that the New Testament view of Jesus is that he is divine and human, there is an end to the matter.

Would that it were so easy! Even if the New Testament does teach that Jesus is fully God and fully human, unless we are able to show that this definition makes some sense, the usefulness of the New Testament teaching is called into question, and the authority of the New Testament thus weakened. Whether the New Testament does teach this is a matter of considerable and ongoing debate. Modern biblical criticism has driven a wedge between the historical words and deeds of Jesus and the interpretation and retelling of these words and deeds in the Gospels. The Chalcedonian fathers may have thought that they were only building on the New Testament foundations, but they did not have the advantage and burden of

modern scholarship; they did not make so clearly the modern
distinction between history and interpretation, or between the
physical/historical realm and the realm of metaphysics and metaphor; they were unaware of the extent to which their interpretation of the New Testament was conditioned by their own non-
biblical philosophical assumptions.

The neat and tidy assumption of many modern traditionalists is
that the Chalcedonian Definition is the product of a long process –
although not necessarily the end-product, as we may have to build
further on the foundations which Chalcedon establishes. Their
view is that we have, as the raw facts, the deeds of Jesus and the
teaching of Jesus about himself: 'I and the Father are one', etc.[4]
Then we have the teaching of Paul about Jesus, based on the
tradition which he received about those deeds and teachings and
on his own experience of the presence and power of the risen Lord
on the Damascus road and subsequently. Paul, it is assumed,
taught clearly that Jesus was God yet human. Subsequently we
have the evangelists and other New Testament writers, who provide the written record of the tradition. They do not express the
philosophical implications of the tradition in any systematized
way, but the beginnings of what will become a systematized
doctrine are present.

In the ensuing three centuries, this view continues, we have a
progressive clarification of these implications, culminating in the
Chalcedonian Definition. No one pretends that Chalcedon is
without problems; everyone concedes that the definition does not
in itself explain how Jesus can be divine, yet possess a human soul
and live in a particular human culture as a particularized man (and
not a woman) of his own time, with all the ensuing limitations that
are inevitably part of this particularization. It is in trying to do
battle with this mystery and to reduce these problems that much
modern christology is concerned, as we shall see. But, so the
argument goes, the Chalcedonian Definition illuminates the inner
logic of the uncodified, unsystematized New Testament christology; it shows us where the New Testament teaching must inevitably lead. The Chalcedonian Definition may not be the whole
truth; since the whole truth is a divine truth it will in any case be
beyond human understanding or expression. But what the Chalcedonian Definition teaches is what the New Testament requires.
Jesus showed himself, and claimed, to be God. The New Testament writers believed this. Chalcedon put this into logical form.
We may try to extend Chalcedon with further elucidation. We

cannot, however, build on any set of foundations other than that provided by Chalcedon.

There are a number of problems with this tidy scheme.

1. The raw facts of Jesus' life and teaching are notoriously difficult to pin down. Even Moule concedes this, though Michael Green seems unaware of this.

> I hold no doctrine of the inerrancy of the New Testament, no brief for the view that every estimate of Christ within it is to be accepted uncritically, simply because it is within the canon.[5]

Modern biblical scholarship has shown us that, operating in all sincerity with a different concept of history from our own, the evangelists have certainly interpreted and recast Jesus' words. Even if we do not go all the way with Bultmann in his doubts about the historicity of the Gospel accounts, few would now argue that all the deeds of Jesus recorded in the Gospels are historically true. Even if they are, the deeds in themselves do not prove his divinity. Miracles, even the resurrection, do not prove that Jesus is God, only that he is an instrument of God. What we are presented with in the New Testament is secondary data. The writers, or at least some of them, thought that Jesus was divine. That is a fact. The primary data – what Jesus himself said or did or his own self-understanding – are not so clear.

We may, of course, still argue that the writers were under the guidance of the Holy Spirit and that their interpretation can therefore be trusted, but we must at least concede that we do not have the undoubted actual words of Jesus. Leslie Houlden says:

> The study of the gospels is far from yielding total scepticism about the Jesus of history, but it remains unclear where exactly accurate information is to be found, and we see that the information is always reflected through the evangelists.[6]

2. Let us grant the argument that Jesus did claim to be God. Does that mean he was necessarily right? The old 'mad, bad or God' argument really cannot hold water. The argument runs thus: to claim to be God, Jesus must have been either insane and possessed of wild delusions about himself; or a very evil person deliberately misleading gullible followers for his own ends; or he must have been right. Such evidence as we have does not in any way support the first two propositions, therefore he must indeed be divine, as he claimed.

Since he did not operate with the clinical preciseness of Greek philosophical terminology, what would Jesus have meant by such a claim? That he spoke with the authority of God, that he acted with the power of God, that he willed what the Father willed? In the Old Testament there are a number of texts which describe the King of Israel in almost divine terms (e.g. II Sam. 7.14a; II Sam. 21.17; Psalm 2.7, 8), but it is clear that the king was not actually regarded as metaphysically identical with God or in any terms approaching the Chalcedonian *homoousios*. Jesus could have envisaged for himself a similar 'Son of God' status without being mad or bad, and we can believe all this about him without agreeing with the Chalcedonian Definition. If Jesus had claimed the right to be worshipped as God that would be another thing. The one thing that as a pious Jew he could not have claimed without blasphemy would have been that. Certainly he is reflected as having been condemned as a blasphemer – see Mark 2.7 and parallels, where he is accused of blasphemy for forgiving sins, or Mark 14.61 and parallels where he is accused of blasphemy for claiming to be the Messiah. There is, however, no New Testament evidence that he invited people to worship him. Indeed he seems to have disclaimed any such right (Mark 10.18 and parallels): 'Why do you call me good? No one is good save God alone.'

3. Jesus, we may argue, may not have claimed the right to be worshipped, but the church in a very short time was indeed worshipping him. Matthew (2.11) says that the wise men 'fell down and worshipped' Jesus. When the word *proskynein* is used, says Heinrich Greeven in Kittel's *Theological Dictionary of the New Testament*, . . . the object is always something – truly or supposedly – divine.[7] Matthew also says that the disciples worshipped Jesus[8] when they recognized him to be the Son of God after a nature miracle. C. S. Lewis argued vigorously that these writers, being closer to Jesus in culture, language, imagery and unconscious assumptions than any modern writer, should have had a better understanding of his nature than is possible for us.[9] He argued further that our scepticism about the reliability of the Gospel records is misplaced, since we have even fewer reliable records about every other figure in ancient history.

Eric Mascall, like C. S. Lewis, argues that however sketchy our historical knowledge of Jesus, as an historical figure he is as well attested as any other figure from ancient history, and he quotes the classical scholar A. N. Sherwin-White to support his point.[10]

Even if this claim is true, it leaves aside the problem that the unconscious assumptions and world-view of people of antiquity may be quite unworkable in our modern culture. Don Cupitt points out that these other figures from ancient history are not the basis of faith, and that therefore the truth of their history is less important.

> Once having adjusted ourselves to the critical view of Jesus, we may realize that he is after all pretty solidly rooted in known history, and we do know something about him, even if not much. Nevertheless, the fact remains that our knowledge of Jesus is not great, and in principle no more than probable. How can something as serious as religious commitment be based on shaky foundations?[11]

Perhaps it is asking too much to insist on historical certainty as a basis for faith. All historical evidence requires selective interpretation, and the interpretation can never be certain. 'Faith' is not 'factual knowledge', but an attitude towards the facts which casts a different light upon them. Mascall's real point is that sceptical biblical scholars reject the divinity of Jesus on *a priori* grounds, and then use the paucity of historical evidence to back their assumptions. He argues that if (with Austin Farrer) we put historical evidence and faith together, then our judgment will be far more positive.

> Thus it is possible through faith and evidence together, and through neither alone, to believe that Christ really and corporeally rose from the dead.[12]

On what, however, is our faith in an historical figure like Jesus to be based, if faith is not derived from historical evidence but is itself a supportive factor to supplement historical evidence? It must be derived from our own experience, which then predisposes us to interpret the historical evidence of the experience of others.

4. Our real difficulty is that the views of the New Testament writers about Jesus are not all the same. They do not understand him to be divine in the same way. Moule does not think that belief in the divinity of Jesus evolved after the New Testament under the influence of Hellenism and Semitic saviour cults. He believes that the very earliest Palestinian church already had a high christology. He also thinks that people experienced Jesus from the beginning as divine, and that this fits the impact that Jesus made on his followers better than the idea that Jesus was initially perceived by his first followers as human, and as divine only as the church became Hellenized.[13] He does not think that belief in Jesus as divine

'evolved' as a result of subsequent extraneous influences, but that it 'developed' from the immediate experience of the disciples and Paul.[14] However, Moule agrees that Paul, with his idea of the corporate Christ into whom we are incorporated, sees Jesus differently from the non-Pauline writers. There is not one uniform New Testament christology; New Testament writers may have all attributed divinity to Jesus, but they did not mean exactly the same thing by that claim.

James Dunn makes the same point:

> . . . within acceptable Jewish Christianity there was diversity; even within the New Testament writings themselves we can see that they do not all represent a single uniform type of faith.[15]
>
> As with Jewish Christianity, so in the case of Hellenistic Christianity [Dunn is referring to Q, Paul and John], we are dealing with a diverse phenomenon.[16]

Thus Dunn concludes

> Christology should not be narrowly confined to one particular assessment of Christ, nor should it play one against another, nor should it insist on 'squeezing' all the different New Testament conceptualizations into one particular 'shape', but it should recognize from the first the significance of Christ could only be apprehended by a diversity of formulations which though not always strictly compatible with each other were not regarded as rendering each other invalid.[17]

If we are to believe these scholars, there is not just one single way of looking at Jesus in the New Testament, not just one way of understanding how it is that he is important for us. New Testament writers have a number of different perspectives, which cannot all be subsumed under one heading. There are a number of different themes or ways of looking at Jesus and at how he affects us. How do we choose the one that is best for us? How do we decide between 'orthodox' or 'liberal' christology?

Houlden suggests that the study of the New Testament reveals that it does not really match with either the Chalcedonian Definition or the looser, more liberal interpretation of Jesus being a special, but human, channel of the divine. In fact, he says, the New Testament writers have very diverse christologies. What they have in common is the conviction that Jesus is the centre of their world; Jesus makes 'all the difference' to them,[18] but since their world views differ, so the way in which Jesus makes 'all the difference' differs too, depending on their own outlook, circumstances, etc. Thus for Paul, the death of Jesus is a sacrifice which achieves reconciliation between humans and God. The resurrection of Jesus achieves a victory over the four tyrants of sin, flesh, law and powers. Christian baptism achieves an incorporation into the fruits of that sacrifice and that victory. The death and resurrection of Jesus are what matters to Paul, more than his life and teaching. For Mark, on the other hand, the life of Jesus is a life of obedience even unto death, a path which we are called to emulate. For Matthew, what makes all the difference is Jesus' teaching of the new Law which is the gateway to our heavenly reward. For John, Jesus makes it possible for us to share in the stable, unchanging, eternal relationship between Father and Son. For the writer of Hebrews, Jesus is the fulfilment of scriptural patterns, particularly the pattern of Yom Kippur.

There is, however, no single interpretation of Jesus and his saving significance in the New Testament. The Chalcedonian Definition is yet another attempt to say how Jesus makes all the difference in a world view shaped by Hellenistic philosophy. It is for us to work out how Jesus makes all the difference for us, in our very different world and circumstances.

Houlden argues that we are now more aware of the origins both of the Chalcedonian Definition and of the scriptural teaching on christology, and that no one can now merely invoke these as if that were the end of the matter.[19] Whereas in the past New Testament studies and patristics provided the agenda for christological study and modern human experience only the material for illustrating these timeless truths, we now need to start from our own experience, as did the New Testament writers, and interpret that experience.[20]

The interaction between New Testament studies and doctrinal theology for which Houlden asks is given monumental expression by Edward Schillebeeckx.[21] Schillebeeckx painstakingly summarizes the views both of biblical exegetes and of doctrinal theologians. In his conclusions he, too, says that, while exegetes differ, it is clear that the New Testament writers write about Jesus with their own presuppositions about human nature and about what it is from which we need salvation, and that the

. . . original experience of salvation in Jesus gets filled out in the gospels with doctrinal and practical problems of the later Christian congregations.[22]

The Gospels, he says, have diverse christologies; there is no single kerygma, or message of good news, behind the Gospels.[23] During Jesus' lifetime he was probably understood as a prophetic figure calling people to obedience to God as part and parcel of his preaching of the kingdom of God.[24] After his death, however, because of what they believed to be ongoing experiences of his forgiveness and his presence, different understandings of Jesus emerge.

What we find is that each successive part of the church turns to Jesus with its different assumptions and needs and world-view, and finds salvation in him.[25] Schillebeeckx traces in the New Testament a number of different 'credal theories' about Jesus: Jesus is the One who will come to usher in the last age; Jesus is the embodiment of the Kingdom of God; Jesus is the suffering Son of Man; Jesus is a *theios aner*, a mighty miracle worker; Jesus is a pious embodiment of wisdom; Jesus is the resurrected Lord.[26] All of these are interpretations of the historical Jesus, the 'factual' Jesus, as each part of the church legitimately seeks to see the relevance of Jesus for their own needs.

This, however, means that in each new age the church can still rightly give new names to Jesus, from the current situation and needs.

> When we take into account the structure that characterizes the 'naming of Jesus' by Christians in the New Testament and the way that structure changes in the light of the continually shifting experience of God's gift of salvation in Jesus, it is clearly in full accord with the gospel for us, with a like experience of salvation, to give new names to Jesus.[27]

Part of the intention of Schillebeeckx's books, as we shall see later, is to build up a picture of Jesus which is compatible with the view of Jesus in the New Testament and in subsequent Christian tradition but is also relevant to the issues of our own period, and compatible with the understanding that we now have of human nature and human well-being. He does not feel himself bound merely to reproduce New Testament or Chalcedonian doctrine. Although he does not use the term, he is embarked on a demythologization programme, endeavouring to get to the heart of the New Testament experience of Jesus and to express an experience of Jesus in our own time which is consistent with that heart but not necessarily with its culturally conditioned expression. In this way Schillebeeckx tries to combine a historical-critical approach to the Bible with dogmatic theology.

5. We cannot follow through the New Testament evidence in detail here. We can only note that some scholars believe that from the beginning Jesus was perceived as divine, while others disagree. Almost everyone concedes that the historical facts about Jesus' life are difficult to reconstruct, although some believe that enough can be established about his life and teaching for this to be a foundation for subsequent interpretation.

Many scholars argue nevertheless that even if we do not know much about the historical Jesus, we do know how the early church perceived him; we have the fact of his impact on the people. Wolfhart Pannenberg argues that whatever our difficulties in expressing what the resurrection means and in reconstructing the historical facts of the appearances of the risen Jesus,

> . . . only the resurrection of Jesus, conceived of in the framework of the cultural situation of primitive Christianity, renders intelligible the early history of Christian faith up to the confessions of Jesus' true divinity.[28]

Pannenberg has his own rich theology about how God can be involved in time and space or in the outworking of human history, all of which has its problems which need not detain us now. Pannenberg is an influential representative, however, of the school which says that the resurrection is a historical event; that it is this that proves the divinity of Jesus; and that we know the resurrection is true because of the faith and courage of the early church, which are inexplicable if the resurrection is not true. Had Jesus not risen from the dead, his claims would have been no more than dreams; but he did rise, and thus is the ultimate revelation of God's purposes, and thus is God.

> . . . if the resurrection of Jesus is certain as an event which really happened, what would that mean? Would it be possible to recognize by this that Jesus was the Son of God, that he was the One who died on the cross for the sins of all men? This is precisely the case.[29]

In its basic form, the argument runs: We cannot be sure how Jesus regarded himself, or how his followers during his lifetime perceived him. We cannot even be sure of exactly what happened at the resurrection; but the transformation in the lives of the disciples, and the growth of the early church, are historical facts which make no

sense unless Jesus did truly rise, and did impart his risen power to
the early church; and this in turn makes no sense unless he is God.
The basis of our faith is thus the experience of the risen Christ in the
church from earliest times until now.

This is not to argue that the resurrection of Jesus in itself proves
that he is God, though Pannenberg seems to suggest this. The
resurrection, if true, only shows that God raised Jesus. Since
Christian belief is that we too shall be raised, this proves no more
than that Jesus was raised first as a kind of first fruits or proto-
resurrection. Thus Pinchas Lapide as a Jew is able to say that he can
accept the historicity of the resurrection of Jesus, indeed that he
thinks the resurrection of Jesus is more probably true than not.[30] He
claims that any Jew of the house of Hillel could say the same. This
does not make Lapide think that Jesus is divine, or even the
Messiah.

> Jesus therefore without doubt belongs to the *praeparatio messia-
> nica* of the full salvation which is still in the future. This does not
> mean that his resurrection makes him the Messiah of Israel for
> Jewish people.[31]

Although some Chalcedonian defendants may have used the
resurrection of Jesus as proof of his divinity, the better argument is
somewhat different. It is that even if the earthly life and miracles
and power of Jesus are not directly accessible to us in history, the
ongoing experience of the power and presence of Jesus in the
church proves that he is God.

Thus Moule can say that there is congruity between the traditional account of Jesus' ministry and the post-resurrection experiences of Jesus in the church. How, he asks, could Jesus have
triggered off such a response if he was not a person of appropriate
magnitude? So Peter Hinchliff argues that the experience of the
presence and power of Jesus long after his human death establishes
the uniqueness of Jesus.

> The uniqueness of Jesus does not simply rest . . . upon the
> character of the historical person (which may not be fully
> recoverable) but upon the undoubted fact that all this 'mytho-
> logy' grouped itself around the historical person. Moreover it
> appeared to be vindicated by the further fact that the claim that
> the faith was communicable seemed to be borne out in the
> experience of subsequent generations.[32]

Not all of those whom I have just quoted are necessarily defending the way that Chalcedon defines the divinity of Jesus; they are only arguing that the experience of the early Christians, and indeed of subsequent Christians, is a historical fact which is accessible to us, and which demands an explanation. Chalcedon is one way of explaining these facts. If we reject that explanation, another is required of us.

There is, however, a weakness in the argument. What these authors claim to be the ongoing power of the risen Jesus in the church could, it seems to me, with equal likelihood be called the ongoing power of God. That is to say, God worked through the human Jesus as far as we can historically establish. God continues to work through those who seek, like Jesus, to be obedient to him. This does not seem to require that Jesus himself be God.

There are many who argue for the historical facticity of the resurrection. Some have argued that the biblical evidence for that facticity is convincing. Others, like Pannenberg, concede that the biblical evidence is confusing and might in any case be *post facto* special pleading, but argue that the vibrant faith, courage, and new power in the early church are inexplicable unless Jesus truly rose. Francis Watson[33] has reviewed these arguments and finds them unconvincing. The Gospel accounts of the resurrection are contradictory; the emergence of the belief in the minds of the disciples is not miraculous nor even all that surprising, given the teaching of Jesus about the coming Kingdom of God in a soon-to-be-realized eschaton or Last Day. The evidence of the courage and new power in the early church depends upon accepting Acts as historical, which is not proven – and indeed there is much internal evidence in the Gospels, if form critics are to be believed, which suggests that the mission of the early church to the Palestinian Jews and the Greeks and Romans was not the success that Luke claims.

This is not to say that the resurrection is proved to be unhistorical either. There may be other reasons for believing in a historical resurrection. Schillebeeckx, for example, argues that only a historical resurrection of Jesus could show us that God is truly on the side of the sufferer.[34] Thus we may believe in the resurrection because '. . . the vision provides a solution to the riddle of the world',[35] and all that is required to permit such a belief is that the historical evidence, such that it is, should not be totally incompatible with such a belief.

If Watson is right – and I am convinced he is – then we are not required to believe that Jesus is God because he rose from the dead.

If we believe that he is God, and rose from the dead, there will be other, probably soteriological, reasons for these beliefs. Belief in the resurrection does not prove Jesus is divine; belief that Jesus is divine leads to a belief in the resurrection. This is not how the New Testament presents its case, of course, but it is arguably how the early church reached its beliefs.

A problem for those who wish to argue that the Christian experience of being filled with power is evidence that Jesus as God is the author of that power is that God seems to work through others also who, following other religions and other ways, do not consciously imitate the path of Jesus. It is common for Muslims to argue that the rapid spread of Islam is proof that Muhammad's message was true. Even if in the church today we share much of the experience of earlier Christians, with different perspectives we may place a different interpretation upon that experience.

6. We have reached the point of saying that ultimately claims for the divinity of Jesus arise out of soteriological factors. People found their lives transformed by Jesus. The only explanation for this, or at least the best explanation, seemed to be that for Jesus to have accomplished that transformation he must be divine, however we choose to express that divinity.

However, we have already had to muddle the tidy pattern of the development of the Chalcedonian Definition outlined above. The pattern is not as neat as we had hoped. We need to observe that even in the centuries leading up to Chalcedon not everyone agreed with its logic. Reading the same scriptures, observing the same phenomenon of lives transformed and of church growth, considerable numbers of pre-Chalcedonian Christians thought that the logical implications of this were different. The majority of Jewish people did not see Jesus as divine. As far as we can tell, the lives of the majority of those who met him in the flesh were not transformed – or at least, they did not become disciples. Of those who did, i.e. the early Christian community, there were many early 'heretics' who believed that logic and experience led them to a different conclusion – though the conclusion varied from adoptionism to docetism. Most of the heretics were probably minority opinions, until we reach the arch-heretic Arius. Although Arius was outvoted at Nicaea, the minority which supported him was a very large one, and it continued to support him even after being shown the 'error' of its ways.

Now of course we may still argue that Nicaea and Constantinople and Chalcedon were right; that their logic is better than that of

Arius, Apollinarius et al.; that they are more true to the New Testament and to church experience. What we cannot do is argue that the Chalcedonian interpretation is self-evidently true to all sincere enquirers.

2

The Chalcedonian Definition

We should examine in more detail the logic of Chalcedon. Despite the fact that the existence of two natures in one person is problematic, Chalcedon argued that however mysterious and difficult to understand, the combination was required. Once the interpretation of Jesus as agent of salvation, as source of power and new life, began to emerge, the early church had to explain both to itself and to outsiders how a human Jesus of Nazarath could be offered worship, *proskynesis*, without supporting a two-God theory. The development of trinitarian belief is not part of my study, beyond saying that the church had to develop this complicated doctrine because it believed that Jesus did have divine status; and it believed that Jesus had divine status because in no other way could its experience of his saving power be explained.[36] Since by this time the predominant thinking in the church was being done by those brought up in Greek culture, particularly that shaped by Platonic thought, it was inevitable that this philosophy would provide the framework.

Christian thinkers believed that our experience of truth in this world is fleeting and ephemeral, but that beyond mundane experience there is a true nature of all things, which we in this life must try to imitate. Thus for Christians there is a true human nature which we must discover and emulate if we are to be saved and liberated. Jesus is therefore one who '. . . is simultaneously paradigm and imitation; he is the "primal image" in which the tarnished *imago Dei*, man, is at the same time restored'.[37]

But if Jesus is the one who shows us the true nature of humanness, and the one who recreates in us the image of God, he is clearly himself the Creator, or so closely associated with the Creator as to be identified with him. How could this be, without ditheism? The debate went on, becoming more and more sophisticated, for more than 200 years. The church was divided between those who believed that Jesus, the Logos or Word, was divine (Johannine christology had superseded the synoptic models of Jesus) and those who believed with the pre-Chalcedonian 'heretic' Arius that to avoid ditheism the Logos must be less than divine. However, it seemed to his opponents that if Arius was correct, their concept of salvation in Jesus lay ruined.

Chalcedon and the preceding councils did not argue that a full incarnational christology was necessary simply for soteriological reasons. Their members believed that the doctrine was required by scripture and by the traditional worship of Jesus in the church. Nevertheless, although the Chalcedonian fathers may not have been fully conscious of the fact, the scriptural and traditional ascriptions of divinity and 'worshipability' to Jesus themselves arose, as I have suggested, for soteriological reasons.

Athanasius, in his *de Incarnatione*,[38] argued thus:

(i) It is God's intention that his purposes in creation should be fulfilled, and fallen humanity saved.

(ii) Human repentance for sin is not enough to secure that salvation, since human nature has become corrupt and the corruption must be cured.

(iii) Athanasius also has the beginning of the theory that sin must be paid for, and that it is beyond human power to make that satisfaction, although in the context he may possibly mean that the payment has to be made to the devil.

> But since the debt paid by all men had still to be paid, for all . . . had to die, therefore after the proof of his divinity given by his works, he now on behalf of all men offered the sacrifice and surrendered his own temple on behalf of all in order to make them guiltless and free from that first transgression.[39]

(iv) Humanity needed to be shown again the true nature of God in whose image humans are made, since that image has become distorted.

(v) Only one who is truly God, and who also becomes truly human, can cure the corruption, pay the debt, and show us the true likeness of God. To be saved we must be recreated into a new being, have the debt due because of sin paid for us, and be taught what humans are meant to be. Only one who is God himself can make a new creation, pay the debt, and give us a true example. Only one who is truly human can do this on our behalf.

(vi) To prove that Jesus is truly God, Athanasius points to the Old Testament promise of a Messiah and Suffering Servant, and claims that no other figure has fulfilled these promises, nor attracted the worship of pagans. He alleges that no other religion, Greek or Jewish, has produced any effective change in people. In Christianity, however, Christian virgins and martyrs prove that the grace of Christ does produce change. Christ's unique healing miracles,[40] in his earthly life and through the church subsequently, also prove his divine power. The successful spread of the gospel; the high moral standard, particularly in sexual matters, of Christian lives;[41] the fact that fierce savages have been converted to ways of peace;[42] all this proves that Jesus is God, and that the incarnation, death and resurrection of Jesus have achieved the redemption of those who turn to Christ.

With regard to the question of how a person can be both divine and human, Athanasius as an Alexandrian bypassed the problem by paying very little attention to the human soul or mind of Jesus. For Athanasius the Incarnation meant that the Logos, the divine Word, the second person of the Trinity, took on a human body rather than human nature. In fact Athanasius did not think that Jesus had a human mind, that he shared our ignorance, or felt our pains.

> Athanasius displays a general tendency to weaken the character of certain of Christ's inner experiences which might be attributed to a human soul.[43]
> Athanasius . . . has admitted the Logos . . . as it were in the place of the soul.[44]

Thus it was very easy for his friend and admirer Apollinarius to deny that Jesus even possessed a human mind, and it was only in the subsequent debate that this issue was grappled with.

What of Athanasius' proofs that Jesus is really God? Hardly any of them could be advanced seriously even by a conservative apologist today. Few scholars would suggest now that the Old Testament authors themselves believed that the promised Messiah or the Suffering Servant had to be divine. Even if Jesus is the fulfilment of these promises, this does not therefore in itself require divinity. So far as evidence for the sanctity of Christian life is concerned, the moral standards of Christian lives are as mixed as any other lives. Certainly there are Christian heroes of purity and sanctity of life – but that is not an apt description of most Christians, and as many heroes could be found amongst followers of other religions. The miracles of Jesus, if historical, can also be matched in many other religions. Colin Brown, who certainly believes in the facticity of the New Testament miracles, is nevertheless clear that the miracles do not in themselves prove the divinity of Jesus, but are part of a 'package'. In Brown's view, the miracles illustrate the teaching of Jesus, and the nature of the God incarnate in Jesus. They are not proofs standing in their own right.[45] Brown, of course, does believe that Jesus was divine and taught of himself that he was divine, but that is another matter. Athanasius' argument from evangelistic success could at some stage or other in history have applied to most of the world religions, certainly Islam and Buddhism – and would be an embarrassment for the church now as it steadily shrinks in membership proportionate to the growth in population.

At the same time, the failure of these 'proofs' is a problem. Athanasius was surely right in expecting that there should be some evidence to which he could point to support his claim that Jesus brings salvation, and if there is little evidence of this kind, the relevance of Jesus is brought into question. This will be something to which we shall return in later chapters.

From Nicaea onwards, Christian consensus has been that Athanasius correctly insisted that an adequate redemption demands an adequate redeemer, and that Jesus is truly, literally, God. Maurice Wiles' questioning of this proposition seems absurdly simple. He makes two criticisms.[46] Athanasius believed that God's intention is for human beings to be restored to non-corruption and to a knowledge of God. They should have the image of God restored in them. Athanasius also assumed that the restorer must himself possess the qualities that he imparts to others. He must himself be incorrupt, perfect, and in full possession of the *imago Dei*. Athanasius assumed this because Plato assumed this. For Plato, something cannot bring into being that which is its opposite. As cold is the opposite of heat, snow cannot bring warmth. Mortality is the opposite of immortality. The soul, since it brings life to the person, cannot itself therefore be mortal; thus Plato believes he has proved the immortality of the soul.[47] By extension Jesus, since he is the bringer of new life, immortality, incorruptibility and divinization, cannot himself be mortal, corruptible, or less than divine.

Wiles points out that although in some contexts it is true that what bestows a quality must itself possess that quality, in many other familiar situations, particularly didactic ones, this is not the case. It is

not necessary for ballet teachers to be themselves virtuoso perfor-
mers. If this were so, no human advance in skill could be possible,
since teachers could not impart that which is beyond their own
achievements.

Perhaps we might counter this by referring to the indwelling Spirit
of God which enables us to surpass ourselves. But Wiles' real
coup-de-grace lies in his second observation. The restoration of
human beings to the image of God, which is what is in Athanasius'
mind when he says that Jesus must needs be divine in order to divinize
us, does not mean that Athanasius thought we should ourselves
become God, but only that we should become restored to innocence
of life and by adoption becoming God's children in his image. If we
are to be adopted as God's children (and if Plato is right about the
qualities necessary in that which bestows), then in order to bestow
adopted sonship upon us, Jesus need be only the adopted son of God.
The saviour who is logically required in order for corruption in
human nature to be cured and for the image of God to be shown forth
once more, is a saviour who is truly human, and who through
obedience and total commitment to God becomes, by God's grace,
an adopted child, the first to be so adopted, one who becomes first
what we hope to become later. A Saviour who is God by nature,
equally divine with the Father, would seem to be precluded, since his
divinity is of a different kind from ours, and therefore cannot be
communicated to us.

Part of Athanasius' point is that if humans are restored to
innocence, this is in effect a new creation, and only God can recreate.
However, it seems equally logical to posit that while the restoration *is*
a new creation, God does this new creating, and Jesus is the first in
this new creation. In that case he would not be a God but a human
being restored to the image of God, and as an obedient servant of
God, a human agent of this recreation.

There is one other aspect of Athanasius' argument, not much
stressed by Athanasius himself, but which in due course would
become the major emphasis in the church's reasons for requiring
belief in the divinity of Jesus: the need for a divine saviour who alone
could pay off the debt of sin. This was to be given its classical
expression in Anselm's *Cur Deus Homo?*[48] We shall examine this in
more detail later. At this point, I will only remark that it is at least
debatable whether a satisfaction theory is really necessary. If,
through grace, true repentance and true amendment is possible, does
God's justice still require the payment of an infinite debt of sin; is his
justice not adequately protected by repentance and amendment?

Athanasius' insistence upon the divinity of Christ was brought sharply into focus during the debate in the church about Arius. Arius' concern was to defend the unity of God; hence his insistence that the Logos was not to be called 'God' except in a purely honorific sense. Since it is not our concern here to enter into the debate about the Trinity, we need only notice that part of the reason for insisting on a trinitarian doctrine arose out of the conviction of the early church that in order to bring salvation, Jesus must be the Logos, and the Logos must be God in the fullest sense. We, however, are beginning to question whether this conviction is necessary.

Having sided with Athanasius against Arius at Nicaea, the pre-Chalcedonian debate moved on to a concern about the unity of the person of Jesus. We have noted that Athanasius and the Alexandrian school generally paid minimal attention to the individual humanity of Jesus. In their eyes, he became Man (i.e. human) rather than 'a man'. Arius would have agreed with them. Whether Jesus had a human soul was not yet a question which had made itself felt.

> It is probably undeniable that in his [i.e. Athanasius'] picture of Christ, the soul of Christ retracts well into the background even if it doesn't disappear completely.[49]

The issue was soon to come to the foreground, however, with the controversy surrounding Apollinarius. Apollinarius said that Jesus did not possess a human soul. The Cappadocians countered that since the human soul was precisely that part of humanness which had become corrupt, unless the Saviour possessed a human soul no salvation could happen. The Council of Constantinople agreed.

Unless one shares with the Cappadocians the strong view of human solidarity which they inherited from Paul and the early church, the arguments both ways seem rather forced. Is there an eternal and unchanging human essence or nature? Were Neanderthals and Cro-Magnons human? This would not be a fair question to pose in retrospect to the early church, but with our more panoramic view of human evolution and development we cannot avoid posing it to ourselves. This is an example of the difficulty of retaining christo-logical definitions framed in a different culture and world view. Can we still believe in an eternal human nature for the Logos to assume?

Why must the Logos as healer assume the nature of the unhealed? Wiles questions whether a doctor needs to become tuberculotic to heal tuberculosis, or a psychiatrist become psychotic to heal the mentally ill. Of course the Cappadocians were not arguing that Jesus became sinful to heal sinners, only that he became human; and their reason for insisting is again the same Platonic conviction that in order to impart a quality, the imparter must itself/himself possess that quality. Jesus imparted restored human nature to us, therefore he must himself possess perfect human nature.

But unless we can give some meaningful content to 'human nature' apart from particularized kind of humans, this belief is vacuous. And if Jesus became merely a *particularized* kind of human – a first-century Jew living in Palestine – and if the Platonic view outlined above is correct, then how is his incarnation relevant to other kinds of humans? Further, how can God become a particular kind of human being without being limited; how can Jesus be fully divine and fully yet 'particularizedly' human? We may argue that because in his humanity he was limited to a particular time and place, he must also be divine in order to be universally relevant to all humanity of all time. We may also argue that although humans differ from age to age, there is still a common thread running through all human life, and that Jesus' life on earth can still be relevant to us now in our different age without his having to be God. The truth is that our concept of human nature, and what would constitute 'perfect' human nature, is as fuzzy as our concept of God, and the problem of a particular person being a universal saviour lives with us still. Neither Chalcedon with its divine Jesus nor the Enlightenment with its Jesus as ideal human person have resolved the problem of what universal or ideal human characteristics are.

Apollinarius was aware of the problem of the particular and the universal, which was why he insisted that Jesus was not fully human but human only in body. Nestorius was aware of the problem, which is why he tried to keep the two natures of Jesus separate. The Council of Chalcedon, influenced by Cyril's fear of a 'two-sons' theory, rejected Nestorius' solution – and it is not clear that Nestorius himself really believed that a separation of the natures in Jesus made sense, or to what extent he shared the two-sons theory of Diodore. Chalcedon quite rightly said that one person, if he is a whole person and not schizophrenic, must have one will. Of course all of us have periods of inner conflict, with two opposing wills pulling us in different directions. But a whole, healthy person has to resolve this conflict.

Chalcedon, then, lays down the limits for the church of what is permissible doctrine. Jesus must be fully human, fully divine, the two natures united in one will. As to how this can be possible, Chalcedon has no answer. Nicaea had already decided that Jesus must be regarded as God. Consideration of the unity of Jesus seemed to demand, therefore, that although he dwelt in a human body he did not have a human soul, since then he would have had two wills, two driving forces in his personhood. However, soteriological considerations led Constantinople and Chalcedon to insist that he did have a human soul. How that soul operated, or what this combination of statements meant in fact, was a problem that Chalcedon shelved for later generations.

3

The Authority of Bible and Councils

In many ways the problem referred to above is more acute than ever for us now, but more of that a little later. If our view is that what general councils of the church have decided is unalterably true, then the problem is just one we have to live with. This is, of course, the situation for many Christians. 'Biblical' Christians argue that if it is in the Bible, it must be true, whatever the logical problems – and human logic is never the equal of God's logic, so one or two problems in comprehending need not worry us unduly. 'Catholic' Christians argue that if undivided councils of the church say it, it must be true, whatever the logical problems. (Of course, exactly which constituted the undivided councils is debated – Roman Catholics would say that Vatican II is an undivided council of the true church.) A cursory knowledge of the history of even those councils leading up to Chalcedon raises questions about how genuinely representative of the churches they were, in view of the jerrymandering and rigging of votes. The Council of Ephesus in 431 CE was an example of the conciliar process at its nadir, but even the Council of Chalcedon was a meeting where 'unholy passions mingled with political ambitions and intrigues were . . . at work'.[50]

There are all sorts of subtleties within these claims for biblical and conciliar authority. Almost everyone concedes a degree of cultural conditioning in their formulations. Because the evangelists believed in a 'three-decker universe' of underworld, world and heaven, that does not mean that even fundamentalist modern Christians share that view. Many traditional Christians would concede that the language of Chalcedon assumes Greek philosophical concepts which we no longer share, and that even the comparison of Greek terms such as *ousia* and *hypostasis* with their Latin equivalents of *substantia* and *persona* led to misunderstandings, as the terms were not exact equivalents. When not only the language but the concepts are translated into, for example, modern English language and culture, the problems are greater still. We may allow for this by insisting that only the essential kernel of the traditional teaching be preserved, and not the philosophical expression of that kernel, which will change from age to age and culture to culture; but whether a naked kernel exists without a philosophical framework is questionable, and determining what is the kernel and what the disposable philosophical husk makes the authority of the conciliar definitions seem at best somewhat unclear.

Nevertheless it would be an injustice and a mistake to regard traditionalists wishing to remain faithful to the Chalcedonian definition as obscurantist. Even though they may insist that the essentials of Chalcedonian christology must be preserved, they do not regard Chalcedon as the final word on the subject. Karl Rahner, for example, says of credal formulae:

> But these derive their life from the fact that they are not the end, but the beginning; not goals, but means, truths which open the way to the – ever greater – Truth.[51]

And Mascall:

> It will be my purpose to argue here that the Definition of Chalcedon is the truth and nothing but the truth, but also that it is not the whole truth.[52]

Mascall goes on to outline a number of questions which Chalcedon does not answer, and which require an answer: how a particular man in a particular set of historical events can be a universal saviour; how Jesus can be divine and yet humanly limited in knowledge; how the incarnation of God in Christ is relevant to other religions. Klaas Runia as a conservative Protestant concedes the ambiguity of the Chalcedonian Definition[53] and that the terms used, or their English equivalents, have changed in meaning over the years.

Nevertheless, traditional Christians still retain the belief that, however mysteriously, Jesus is fully God and fully man, and they believe that if this mystery is abandoned, the experience of Christ in the church over the centuries will be denied or at least truncated.

It is important to take tradition seriously. Every new age has its own insights and every age its own blindnesses. There is a real danger that if with twentieth-century arrogance we reject traditional formulations as being disproved by modern knowledge, we shall be slaves of this blindness. There is a suitable humility in conceding that, even though such formulations may seem to us to be more mystery than enlightenment, another and later age may perceive again truths that at present are impenetrable for us. The insights of the past need to be taken seriously as the ground and springboard of our own understanding. Wiles himself argues that in part the test of the truthfulness of our own reformulations will be the extent to which they preserve the genuine insights of the past.[54] There is always some similarity between present and past situations, a certain perennialness about human nature. John Macquarrie's formative factors in theology[55] include tradition along with experience, revelation, scripture, culture and reason, and 'theology must hold a nice balance or tension among the formative factors'.[56] Macquarrie does not say whether these are equal factors, nor what one does if they lead one to contradictory conclusions – that is, if tradition and reason seem to clash. Elsewhere[57] Macquarrie refuses to defend traditional Christian belief on fideistic grounds. Our doctrine of Christ must be true to what we know of his history and his historical effects, and to our experience of things as they actually are. Our experience of truth is an inward, subjective, intuitive apprehension, which we then with some inevitable clumsiness try to express verbally.

Wiles says that doctrine is the intuitive combination of scripture, tradition, prayer and liturgy with reason and common sense, but that in the final outcome doctrine must be coherent: it must make sense, and hold all these factors together in a logical way. He also pleads, sensibly, for economy or parsimony, seeking for what the evidence requires us to say in the most economic way, not for what the evidence will allow us to say.[58]

In our own reformulation of doctrine, then, we cannot disregard what scripture and tradition say about Jesus. What we find in fact is that both scripture and tradition say many things about Jesus. We need to ask ourselves why they say what they do, what their experience was that led them to say this, whether it matches our own experience and makes sense. Those things which seem to us to contain logical fallacies, or to be inconsistent with our own experience, we will not reject out of hand, for it might be our own limitation of knowledge and experience which make it impossible for us at present to understand – but we will put such things aside as not being useful at present. Stewart Sutherland says of his own revisionary approach that:

> There is much that has been central to that tradition which I shall either discard or leave on one side like an engine idling in neutral gear with apparently no role to play in the affairs of life.[59]

Perhaps on the other hand Schillebeeckx is right when he says that despite the great cultural changes between the time of the New Testament and Chalcedon, or between Chalcedon and us, there is always still some link or connection with what went before.

> Chalcedon . . . has something meaningful to say, while . . . it may irritate and alienate.[60]

Since Schillebeeckx sits somewhat lightly to the Chalcedonian Definition, however, he is interpreting 'meaningful' rather widely. Clearly the church of Chalcedon, like the church of the New Testament, bore witness to the truth that Jesus was, in their experience, the source of their own salvation. As I ask myself whether, and how, Jesus is the source of salvation now, I shall argue, with Wiles, that it is our own reason and experience which must be the final arbiter of what we choose from scripture and tradition as being useful at present, while we try to be open to and to understand the experience of those who have gone before us. It is our reason and our reasoned interpretation of our own experience that is normative, not scripture or tradition. Just because scripture or traditional formulations say something does not alone make that normative doctrine – and I defend this stand partly on the grounds that neither scripture nor tradition has a single doctrine of Jesus; rather, they present us with a number of different insights, from which we have to choose. However, those concepts which we find contrary to our own reason and experience we do not reject, but merely put aside. For the present, we need to work only with those insights which are consistent with a logical, economical interpretation of our own experience, building upon insights from the past.

Brian Hebblethwaite says of Wiles' concept of parsimony that while he does not disagree with it, the concept should not be used in a restrictive way.

> My objection is not to the criterion of economy as such . . . my objection rather is to stress an economy to the neglect of comprehensiveness.[61]

He concedes that we cannot hold a doctrine in the face of contradictory evidence, but that we should not limit ourselves to believe only what the evidence requires.

> . . . we need to beware of thinking that historical evidence alone must be seen to necessitate such an interpretation before we can allow ourselves to accept it.[62]

I think we need to go a little further than this. Much of the doctrine handed on to us from the past will not be contradictory to what can be proved by historical evidence, but will not be required by that evidence either. Does that mean we should continue to believe everything from the past, unless it is proved to be untrue? Hebblethwaite argues that since those arguing within the church live in a tradition, they cannot abandon that position unless it is proved false.[63] Alister McGrath argues the same point at greater length.[64]

I am not arguing for restriction of belief to that which is consistent with hard evidence; but traditional belief did not emerge in a vacuum. It arose out of the socially and culturally conditioned experience of our forebears. If our own socio-cultural environment no longer requires the same interpretation as that of our forebears, or if we no longer have that experience, the specific belief in question will not be usable by us. We may not be able to prove that it is not true. Indeed, we should keep an open mind lest a wider experience or a broader understanding shows us that there is a reason for the belief after all. Without some comparable experience, however, and without some shared understanding of the nature of that experience, the belief cannot really work for us.

Hebblethwaite points out that many traditional doctrines – the creation, the Fall – have had to be restated in a different way in the light of new knowledge and evidence, without abandonment of these doctrines,[65] and suggests that the doctrine of the Incarnation can likewise survive. This is only true, however, if by 'survive' we mean in a radically changed form. The doctrine of creation can fairly easily be restated in evolutionary terms without loss. The doctrine of the fall surely cannot. We can no longer easily believe in a literal fall. To say '. . . the doctrine of the Fall is more profoundly grasped when it is articulated in terms of the radical gap between human achievement and the divine purpose.'[66] is to say that 'fall' does not literally mean fall, but a falling short. The doctrine then is no longer about a state of human perfection once existent but now lost. We may still have a doctrine of human falling short, but it does not mean what it once did. To say 'the doctrine of the Incarnation is more profoundly grasped when it is articulated in terms of human kenosis' is surely to invite a similar response. It represents a considerable change from what the doctrine of Incarnation once meant. Liberal Christians may then put forward a concept of Incarnation suggesting that Jesus is a human agent of God rather than being himself ontologically divine, without being charged with disloyalty to inherited tradition. They surely have as much warranty to do this as has Hebblethwaite to put forward his radically revised fall or kenotic incarnational theories.

We need, then, to find the interpretation that fits our own experience, and that part of the experience of our forebears with which we can still identify, as logically and as economically as possible. Mascall, for example, quotes extensively from the works of modern French christologists to show that it is logically possible to believe that Jesus is divine without denying his true humanity, with sophisticated arguments about the nature of human consciousness.[67] His intention is to show that the mystery of christological doctrine does not mean that it is illogical or nonsense. Using Wiles' principle of economy or 'parsimony', I shall be suggesting that this effort is not really useful. Later in this book, I shall explore our own experience and interpretation of salvation, and I shall be suggesting, in the light of that exploration, how I can best understand what 'salvation' means. I will be suggesting further that for this concept of salvation to work, there is not the same logical necessity for Jesus to be 'consubstantial with the Father', equally divine with the Father. A humanly obedient Jesus makes more sense to us, is more true to our experience and our interpretation of the evidence, and still provides the salvation that we need. A principle of economy in explanation must lead us to choose the simpler explanation. The unresolved mystery of Chalcedon as to how in one person a fully divine and a fully human nature can be united is, on this argument, an unnecessary mystery.

There is, however, an inevitable degree of tentativeness about this judgment. Subsequent experience and reinterpretation may show that salvation does mean what Anselm or other traditional theorists have suggested, and that a logical *sequitur* is that Jesus is, after all, both divine and human. At that point, Mascall's arguments become useful again. For the present, I shall suggest[68] that the most coherent view of salvation does not require us to believe that Jesus is both divine and human, and that the belief is therefore an unnecessary complication which makes the practice of religion more difficult.

4

Modern Problems with Chalcedon

Our understanding of the world, of human nature, and of the history and place of humans in the world, even our understanding of the Bible and the New Testament, has changed since Chalcedon. Because inevitably our understanding of God is linked with our understanding of ourselves and of the world, the concept of God has changed too – if in no other respect than that events which in a prescientific era could only be explained by the direct agency of God are now seen to have their own causation within the natural laws of the universe. Christological doctrine is affected by our understanding of God, of human nature, and of the world. A number of ways in which our understanding has changed are set out below.

They amount to the implications for christology of modern science, modern psychology, modern biblical criticism, and modern (or at least post-Aristotelian) philosophy. The term 'the Enlightenment' is used in this book in a very generalized sense to refer to all ,those, from the Cambridge Platonists on, who claimed to prefer reason to dogma. Following the trauma of Reformation and Counter-Reformation, with the associated massacres, inquisitions, burnings, all in the name of religion, there was a fairly general tendency from the late seventeenth century onwards to stress the value of each individual's reason. Scientific advances from Newton through Darwin to Einstein made it seem as though the real key to discovering truth lay not in theology but in the empirical sciences. The supernatural, the miraculous, were all suspect. Hume and Kant had shown that the traditional proofs for God's existence from cosmology or teleology were shaky. The very existence of God was questioned – though not so much in public, for fear of reprisals. The traditional sources of revelation were seen to be the products of human rather than of divine agency. The human element in the authorship of the Bible was increasingly recognized. The human element in the formulation of church doctrine had become all too apparent, as Catholic spokesmen and the various rival reformers all made their differing claims to speak with the authentic Christian voice. Colonial expansionism brought Europe back in touch with the great world religions, so that the cultural relativity of particular religious doctrines became clearer, as well as the fact that wisdom and virtue were to be found outside as well as within the church. There was no one single philosophical outlook that dominated the scene, as Platonism and Aristotelianism had done successively in earlier generations. There was no longer one single Christian voice either; separated churches taught diverse and contradictory doctrines. But into this vacuum of uncertainty, a claimant for renewed optimism and certainty was offering its comforts. There was great optimism about the power of human reason, aided by human discovery about the world in which we live. The human conscience, too, could discern right from wrong without the necessity of imposed dogma. If all followed their reason and conscience, then the potential for the human race was boundless, provided that the merchants of obscurantism – church, monarchy, overweening state – were kept in check.

Within the Enlightenment as I have defined it there were different views. Not all Enlightenment or post-Enlightenment thinkers shared all these features. Nor would we necessarily agree with all of them ourselves. Modern scientific indeterminism – the conflicting wave/particle theories are usually offered as an example of this point – means that Newtonian positivism about the models of physics no longer hold. Some philosophers tentatively defend again the Thomist and even Anselmian views for God's existence. After two world wars, the holocaust and the threat of nuclear destruction, it is hard to maintain unmixed optimism about the advance of the human race.

It is true, as well, that the philosophers of the Enlightenment had their own unconscious cultural biases. Their rigid exclusion of all that they regarded as supernatural we suspect to be as arbitrary and doctrinaire as the views of those whom they opposed. After all, the validity of a decision to discount any evidence or experience but that derived from the empirical senses is notoriously unable to be proved on empirical grounds. Alvin Plantinga[69] with his notion of basic and

properly basic beliefs has made a possible case for the equal, or even
superior, validity of traditional theism. With regard to biblical
authority, by no means all modern biblical scholars would share the
extreme scepticism concerning the New Testament records of the
nineteenth century reconstructers of the 'Lives of Jesus'.

Nevertheless for all this, biblical scholarship, even of a conservative nature, makes it virtually impossible for us to regard the Bible
as a source of revelation in exactly the same way as before. Modern
scientific knowledge may have its indeterminacies, but at a micro-
rather than a macro-level. We can no longer revert to an earth-
centred view of the universe, or to a naive creationism, or to belief
in an unhistorical Garden of Eden, or to a pre-Freudian view of
human nature. Between ourselves and the world of Archbishop
Ussher[70] there is a great gulf fixed.

> Ours is the post-Enlightenment world, however fragmented and
> pluriform we find that world to be, and however critical of that
> world we may become. There have been changes of permanent
> significance since ancient and mediaeval times.[71]

So we set out to look at some of these changes.

1. Maurice Wiles[72] suggests that it is arguable that the Chalcedonian Definition arose as much out of the fathers' understanding of
creation as out of soteriological considerations. Patristic belief
generally, if we exclude Irenaeus, was that God created Adam and
Eve, literally the forebears of the human race, in a state of
perfection. Paradise was a brief golden age. Adam and Eve were
perfect human beings, possessing superhuman powers, blessed with
superhuman knowledge, and possessing immortality by nature.
With the fall, all was lost. Human power and knowledge
became more limited; immortality was lost. In order to restore
humans to their proper destiny, God had to recreate humanity
through a new Man – and, since the divine Logos was the agent of
God in the first creation, it was necessary that the Logos be the
agent of the new. Thus, the Logos became the new Man.

There is already a problem in this scenario, implicit even in Paul.
Belief in a literal Adam and Eve makes it possible to understand
how humans are one with Adam and his fall. We would be Adam's
descendents, we would share his genes, we would have, perhaps, a
shared 'family' responsibility. But how do we explain the solidarity
of Christians with Jesus as their new Adam? There is no genetic
link. Paul uses the imagery of dying and rebirth in Christ, but
exactly what that means is problematic, as even Moule concedes.

Biological solidarity with Adam was (for Paul) a fact; mystical solidarity with Christ is a metaphysical theory.

Few Christians now believe in paradisal humanity as a literal historical fact. We may explain the Fall as the cumulative effect of generations of human sin, but we no longer believe that there ever was an original man who was perfectly good, with all the super-human powers of the traditional Adam. We may want to argue that Neanderthal humanity had a certain naive moral innocence, but that is beside the point. Early Christian belief did not see Jesus as the new Neanderthal. It makes more sense for us to see in Jesus a prototype of future humanity than a recreation of a past Adamic figure. Thus salvation for us is not a reaching back into the past, a recreation of that which had become marred, but a reaching forward into the future. In that respect our understanding of salvation is of necessity radically different from that of Chalcedon.

It would be untrue to say that all the pre-Chalcedonian Fathers thought the same about Adam, although of course they all believed that Adam was literally the forefather of the human race. Irenaeus, although he believed that Jesus was a recapitulation of Adam, also believed that Adam himself was '. . . morally, spiritually and intellectually a child', who because of his '. . . very weakness and inexperience . . .' was almost bound to fall into sin.[73] Adam was not perfect Man.

Irenaeus could not be expected to understand fully the force of his own argument. In a post-Freudian age, however, we know that the human will is determined by more than the power of reason. Our understanding of things, and the decisions we take in the light of that understanding, are inevitably flawed not only because our rational and moral knowledge is imperfect, like Irenaeus' Adam, but by the unconscious effect upon us of environment, upbringing, childhood experiences and many other factors which we do not understand. This is what it means to be human. There never was a human being who could make perfectly rational decisions unaffected by these extra-rational factors.

If Jesus was fully human, the same must have applied to him. His knowledge and power must have been human, and therefore limited and imperfect. Scholastic theologians could talk about Jesus in his human knowledge possessing infused knowledge as well as experiential, learned knowledge. Rahner and some other contemporary theologians reinterpret this and talk of Jesus' prereflective, primordial consciousness of himself and his world. Nevertheless, as Gerald O'Collins concedes, there must have been real limitations in the knowledge of the human Jesus.[74] A pre-reflective knowledge is not the same as a fully reflective, fully interpreted knowledge, and is really, in Rahner's own terms, only an openness, a sort of vague hunch (a 'Vorgriff'), towards that full knowledge and understanding.

This is a particular problem for traditional theism with its belief in the omnipotence and omniscience of God. How can Jesus be omnipotent and all-knowing and yet truly human? The kenoticists[75] in varying degrees of sophistication from Thomasius of Erlangen to Vincent Taylor tried to suggest ways in which the incarnate God in Jesus divested himself of these 'omni-s'. Their critics pointed out that this implies change in God, which for traditional theism is out of the question. If, rather, we wish to say with Taylor that these 'omni-s' are latent but still present during the Incarnation, and that God has therefore not changed in his nature but only in his relationship with the world, this comes close to meaninglessness. If latent, how are the divine qualities in Jesus present in any meaningful way? What can latent omniscience mean? However, since clearly some kenosis is nevertheless absolutely necessary if the humanity of Jesus is to be any kind of true humanity, critics like Brunner have said that kenotic theory errs in trying to explain the human psychology of the God-man, which by its nature must be mysterious and impenetrable to us.

> We can only understand [the self-consciousness] of Jesus rightly if we understand it not psychologically but purely positively.[76]

In what way the divine consciousness of the Son functions while he is incarnate is not revealed to us.

Thus Mascall suggests,

> It is, I suggest, futile for us to try to guess what it feels like to be God incarnate.[77]

Brian Hebblethwaite believes that some kind of kenotic theory is necessary if Jesus is to be seen as truly human.

> In no way do we follow the 'docetic' tendencies of early Christianity, which found it hard to believe . . . that Jesus shared the limitations of human psychology and cognition.[78]

Hebblethwaite, while regarding himself as a defender of Chalcedonian orthodoxy, still says

> It is highly implausible for us in the light of informed and critical
> study of the New Testament, as well as of philosophical and
> psychological realism about what it is to be a man, to suppose that
> Jesus knew himself to be or thought of himself as divine.[79]

Thus Hebblethwaite grants that our christology needs to be
adapted, not only because of the assault of post-Enlightenment
views about human nature, but also because of the findings of
biblical criticism. However, he thinks that recognition that the
human Jesus must have had limitations of psyche and knowledge
does not rule out belief in Jesus as God and human, because we
know so little about the nature of God or of human nature.[80] Also,
since humans are made in the image of God, there is no alien
incompatibility between divine and human nature.[81] Despite his
human limitations, the divine authority, power, and effect upon
people still shines through in Jesus.[82]

However, as soon as Hebblethwaite comes to consider how Jesus
can have had a human consciousness and yet be God, we seem to
revert, as with Mascall, to mystery once more.

> It is at this point that we must remember that we are struggling to
> speak of the infinite, internally differentiated being of God,
> whose own eternal love, given and received within the Trinity, is
> mirrored in the love of Jesus for the Father.[83]

If Jesus is divine, then it must be true that his self-consciousness will
be mysterious and largely unknowable to us. I agree with Mascall
that our own self-knowledge is mysterious enough, so that the
addition of additional mystery is not in itself unacceptable. I agree
with Hebblethwaite's observations that many liberal theologians
have a concept of God which is just as paradoxical and problematic
as the divine/human concept concerning Jesus,[84] so that Chalcedonian refuge into mystery is not a closed-shop activity. Thomas
Morris shows that a kenotic concept could be defended as not being
illogical. He prefers a different approach by means of which to show
that Jesus can be omnipotent and yet operate with a human mind.[85]
A kenotic approach, for Morris, has too weak a concept of the
immutability of God, and deals unsatisfactorily with the modalities
of divine attributes. Nevertheless, for Morris, if his own two-minds
theory should be shown to be untenable, the kenotic approach
would not be illogical. The question is whether it is in fact necessary.
The mystery certainly makes an understanding of Jesus less
attainable for us. If we stay with Wiles' principle of economy – that

we do not bring into our explanation extra complications which are not required – then the struggles of the kenotic school are beside the point, unless we are shown that a less than fully divine Jesus has no soteriological significance for us. We shall give our attention to this later.

The problem is compounded for us once we take into account the environmental and developmental factors raised by modern psychology. Jesus, as a human person, must have been influenced by unconscious cultural factors. He must have shared not only the limitations of knowledge of his time but also the prejudices and moral blindnesses. Not to have done so would mean that he did not have a human personality, since this is at least partly how personality is formed. Human personality does not exist in a vacuum, but exists in relationship to other persons, who affect and change the person that I am.

Indeed there is possible scriptural evidence that Jesus did have moral blindnesses and cultural prejudices. His reported vituperative attitude to the Pharisees[86] was, in the light of our understanding of Pharisaic teaching, unjustified. If Vermes is to be believed, much of Jesus' teaching is what the Pharisees themselves taught. The Pharisees were not the hypocritical 'whited sepulchres' of the Gospels, and though 'there is little doubt that the Pharisees disliked his non-conformity and would have preferred him to abstain from healing on the sabbath where life was not in danger',[87] the Pharisees themselves approved of suspending sabbath rules in order to save life. For them every part of life was invested with religious significance, so that the minutiae of religious observance were important as they seem not to have been for Jesus. Jesus' lack of empathy with the reasons for Pharisaic attention to detail may be seen to be understandable in the light of his human attempts to reform Judaism, but is lacking in the balance and fairness we would expect of a divine being.

Jesus seems also to have shared the Jewish xenophobia of the time. His interchange with the Syro-Phoenician woman,[88] his initial reluctance to help her, his rudeness in addressing her as a dog, is an embarrassment. He seems as a teenager to have shown a typical self-centredness in his absorption with his own affairs and his own dignity to the exclusion of any understanding and concern for his parents in their natural worry when he went missing for three days.[89] He seems to have shared the male chauvinist prejudices of his time in his manner of address to his mother.[90] He even seems to have made a human error of judgment in including Judas amongst his twelve closest companions.

Looked at from a human perspective, none of this need worry us. He seems to have learned from his mistakes. He did, after all, befriend a Pharisee in Nicodemus. He was impressed by the Syro-Phoenician woman's persistence and courage and changed his attitude to her. He made provision for his mother's welfare from the cross. None of these initial limitations in his attitude are culpable – all are fully explained by factors such as immaturity, upbringing and cultural conditioning. For humans, not only cognitive knowledge but morality and values have to be learned through experience. Any moral immaturity in Jesus, however, makes it more difficult to understand what is meant by saying that Jesus is God, though if Morris' two-minds theory is accepted, the problem is not logically insuperable. Nevertheless, the necessary logical argument becomes more and more complex, and less parsimonious.

Of course, since we have raised caveats about the historicity of some of the Gospel stories, and since certainly some of these stories come from what the form critics would regard as legendary material, perhaps these accounts are not historically accurate. Perhaps Jesus' prejudices against the Pharisees are really the prejudices of Matthew's church community. But if Jesus was truly human, some such blindnesses and errors must have happened, or else he did not develop in a truly human way. Thus whether or not the scriptural accounts are historical is not material to the point.

Perhaps it is a mistake to think that Jesus' humanity, his growth in knowledge and consciousness and moral values, was like our own? Stephen Sykes suggests that liberal Christians are illogical. They want Jesus to be fully human like us for soteriological reasons – for if his life is not human, how can his life be of relevance to those of us who are human? – and they think that a human Jesus who is also divine is not like us. But unless Jesus is unique, is different from us, Sykes asks how he can save us anyway.

> But this is the exact point of the greatest difficulty. If we deny that there is anything remarkable about Jesus, if Jesus really was an ordinary fallible human being and no more, then our Christology has no basis in fact . . . Can Jesus both be ordinary *and* a climacteric?[91]

Mascall makes much the same point.[92] If these critics are right, liberal Christians are in a cul-de-sac. They cannot have a purely human Jesus who is also a saviour. Hebblethwaite develops the point further: liberal Christians cannot easily have a Jesus who is humanly conditioned and who is not divine, but who is still of universal human significance.[93]

Sykes does not underestimate the contrary problem of understanding a Jesus who is both divine and human. In fact he adds further dimensions to it. He asks whether Jesus was ever childishly selfish and harsh – and if not, was he a truly human child? Was his consciousness a masculine self-consciousness? And if not, how was he a true man? And yet, if his consciousness was that of a man rather than that of a woman, how is his incarnation of relevance to women? Nevertheless, in Sykes' view, for soteriological reasons we must, in faith if not in full knowledge, claim that Jesus was at every stage of his life perfect with a perfection that befits that stage; he was not merely like us, or else his life is irrelevant to us, and he is not a Saviour. We are back with the same issue: it is difficult to understand how Jesus can be God and man, but we must accept the mystery as a concomitant of salvation.

Schillebeeckx points out that from Lessing and the Enlightenment on, people have assumed that Jesus' relevance to us is that he enables us to reach a truer humanity or 'humanum' – but that the nature of the humanum is not necessarily clear to us.

> Our age has come to see that mankind does not have at its beck and call this humanum; what is truly worthy of man is not something we all know and have within our power.[94]

The nineteenth-century liberals perhaps deserve Sykes' rebuttal. It is always dangerous to decide what the truth is on *a priori* grounds and then interpret the evidence to suit the truth. Like the deists before them, the many Life of Jesus authors in the nineteenth-century had already decided that miracles were impossible, the virgin birth out of the question; that to be human meant to be just like themselves – and then had to face the challenge as to why they bothered with such a Jesus at all.

Our view of what it is to be human now is not quite the same as it was in the nineteenth century. The factors which we are discussing in this chapter were beginning to make themselves felt then but are now much clearer. I shall suggest that in view of these factors it is more difficult for us to make sense of Jesus as fully divine. I am not, like the nineteenth-century liberals, ruling this out *a priori*. If it can be shown, as Chalcedon and Christians throughout the ensuing centuries believed, that unless Jesus is divine no salvation is conceivable, then I will concede that Mascall's pointers to the work of the French christologists, and their efforts to show how Jesus could conceivably have been God and yet possess a properly human consciousness, and Sykes' suggestion (with many others) that it is possible in faith to make some sense of the mystery of the human/ divine nature of Jesus, would all be helpful. I shall be suggesting later in this book, however, that traditional views of salvation are not the most useful or relevant ways of understanding salvation in view of the problems which face humans today, and that with a different concept of salvation, we no longer need the same emphasis on the divinity of Jesus. If this is indeed the case, then the factors to be discussed in the following paragraphs become more decisive.

2. Cupitt makes the point [95] that we cannot be as human-centred in our view of the cosmos as was once the case, nor as grandiose in our concept of human importance. In the cosmos, the earth is a tiny and transient entity, with a very brief history in cosmic terms. The period over which humans have been present in that brief history is infinitesimal. To believe that the incarnation of God as a man is of cosmic significance is harder to accept than it was. Paul's 'whole creation groaning and travailing' until Jesus sets it free (Rom. 8.22) seems a somewhat aggrandized notion. We shall see below that even the much reduced concept of Jesus as being of universal human significance is not without difficulty. To say he is of cosmic significance is harder still.

Thomas Morris says that the cosmic insignificance of humanity is not such a new concept. He quotes Psalm 83.4 to make his point:

> They [the enemies of God] say, 'Come, let us wipe them out as a nation; let the name of Israel be remembered no more!'

He says that it is not necessarily true that smallness, or newness, implies insignificance. [96] Cupitt is following Thomas Paine or Ralph Waldo Emerson in concluding that the vastness of the cosmos renders Christian claims arrogant or anthropocentric; but in fact the significance of humanity lies, for the theist, purely in the fact that God has chosen humans for his purposes. The existence of other worlds or other aeons of time before humanity appeared on the scene is no argument for denying the centrality of human destiny in God's plans.

The possibility of other rational beings in other worlds raises the problem of human incarnation again. Paul and Linda Badham argue that it is statistically likely that there are countless millions of planets where there is, has been, and will be, rational life. Either such beings have not sinned, in which case humans are surely of less importance and value than they are, or more likely (since, for the

Badhams, like Schleiermacher, sin is a virtually inevitable result of living in a physical world), they have sinned, in which case God must have been redemptively incarnate in all these millions of planets. Since the planets exist in time, even if God does not, there is no time for God to be successively incarnated in them all. Thus, say the Badhams, the received ideas about both incarnation and atonement need to be substantially revised.[97]

This may seem a very speculative, pernickety argument, since we do not know for certain that any such rationally inhabited planets occur. Also, traditional theology has always believed in the existence of sinless angels without that cutting across belief in the specialness of humans. The matter is easily resolved by saying that God simply chose to love humans specially. Morris shows that multiple, even simultaneous, incarnations, if shown to be theologically necessary, are not logically impossible. To put it rather roughly, if Morris is right and Jesus possessed simultaneously and distinctly a divine and a human mind[98] and this constitutes the Incarnation, there is no logical reason why he cannot possess simultaneously a divine + human + Martian + Venusian (or whatever) mind, incarnate on earth and Mars and Venus and however many more planets are required, all at the same time.

Nevertheless, while an anthropocentric view of the world may be logically possible, and while a full incarnational christology is thus not ruled out, it must surely be conceded that these views are made somewhat more problematic, somewhat less self-evidently true, than was earlier the case. Pre-Copernican anthropology fits more easily with the idea of God becoming uniquely incarnate in human form. Even if we may claim no more than this, it makes it more important to show why traditional incarnational views are still the best way to explain our present combination of knowledge and experience.

3. Biblical criticism has brought about two rather contradictory results. On the one hand we are more keenly aware that there are a number of different theologies operating in the New Testament and not one single overriding view. We have also become aware that the theological interests of the New Testament authors and of the early church which was the cradle of the New Testament have coloured and shaped their account of the historical Jesus. What seemed in the past to be the teaching of Jesus himself turns out in many cases to be the reflective teaching of the post-resurrection church. The authority of the New Testament has been weakened, or at least been shown to have a greater human element than was earlier realized.

On the other hand, careful use of the tools of biblical criticism has enabled us to build up something of a more reliable picture of the historical Jesus. Although most scholars would concede that these results are tenuous, the picture of Jesus which emerges is, while attractive, a very human picture: a prophetic figure, affected by the cultural and historical viewpoint of his own people, shaped by the rabbinic tradition, with a deep love of God and a sense of the closest personal intimacy with him.

He seems to have been subject to many of the same failings that any growing human person experiences – childhood self-centredness, male chauvinism, ethnic closedness. He made mistakes. He predicted, it seems, an early parousia, that is, that he would return along with the general resurrection of humankind in the very near future. When the Epistle to the Hebrews says that he was tempted as we are,[99] we can understand that to mean not only external temptation, but the inevitable limitation and conditioning that is part of being a human person of a particular age and stage of development. This is not to say that Jesus sinned in any culpable way; of that we have no knowledge. It does, however, imply an imperfection, not culpable, that is part of being human. When the Cappadocians said that what is unassumed is unhealed, they necessarily implied a sharing in these imperfections which are part of the human lot.

This does not seem to be reading back into the synoptic Gospels a modern humanistic understanding. These elements are present in all these Gospels, alongside other strands. Some of them are present even in the Gospel of John with its far more explicit Logos Christology. And certainly Hebrews says that Jesus 'learned' obedience and 'was made' perfect.[100]

4. The point was made earlier that we no longer believe in a literal Eden and a literal pair of human forebears. The idea of Jesus as the New Adam, so important to Athanasius, has therefore to be seen as a mythical concept, having a certain evocative or poetic truth but not as the basis of a factual statement. To the extent that Athanasian doctrine builds on this mythology as fact, it can no longer hold water. This has some consequences.

I have argued that the human nature of Jesus must have involved him in cultural conditioning, contingency, the limitation of knowledge and of moral maturity. I shall be arguing below that to understand Jesus as human, we would need to understand him as being able to make autonomous decisions, and to be able even to choose sin. We shall also be exploring the implications of the human suffering of Jesus. For us, to be limited and conditioned and subject to error and uncertainty and pain is part of the human situation.

Because of their belief in paradisal Adam, for the early church these conditions of the human situation were seen as part of sharing in a *fallen* human nature. Jesus, for them, could be truly human, truly Adam-like though even more perfect, without any of these limitations, because he was not fallen, since the first Adam was without these limitations. The option of this understanding is not open to us. We may still argue that Jesus was 'human-as-humanity-will-be', that he was the living example of a perfected man; but, if he was truly human, he must have reached that point of perfection through sharing in and overcoming all the limitations, for human knowledge and human values are learned knowledge and learned values. Thus if we wish to say that he is and always was God (that is, not that he became perfect but that he was perfect from the beginning), we shall have to show how divine perfection can subsist together with contingency, pain, emotional immaturity, the possibility of error and of sin.

Morris points out that to say that all human beings in our experience are culturally conditioned, limited in knowledge, liable to sin, etc., does not necessarily entail that these qualities are essential to human nature. The fact that they are common, or even universal, except for Jesus only means that 'mere' humanity includes these limitations. 'Full' humanity need not. He refuses to accept that there is anything indefensibly illogical about the traditional docrine of the Incarnation. He believes that with his 'two-minds' approach we can show how divine perfection can subsist together with contingency, limitation in knowledge, openness to sin, and the other limitations of 'mere' humanity.

I discuss below[101] some possible problems with Morris's approach. Even if he is right, it must be clear that our modern understanding of what it is to be human is in important ways different from that of Chalcedon.

5. When Christians believed in Adam as a literal forefather of the human race, it was logical to see Jesus as the New Adam, and all those who were not incorporated into Jesus as still being lost and banished from Eden along with the old Adam. Since we no longer share the old belief about a literal single ancestor, the logic no longer works. The heart of New Testament belief in the solidarity of the human race has been excised.

Christians have come now to have moral qualms about excluding other religions from salvation. Sutherland[102] has said that we cannot accept as religiously true anything which runs counter to our moral convictions. Orthodox Christianity used to teach – and many still believe it to be true – that since forgiveness of sin was possible only because Jesus had died for our sins, and since the effect of Jesus' vicarious sacrifice had to be accepted by faith to be efficacious, then only those who had accepted Jesus as Lord and Saviour (however that acceptance was understood) could be saved. But it is surely morally outrageous to believe that God will condemn over half the present population of the world to eternal damnation because they are not Christian. Few would now feel able to argue with Hugh of St Victor that the damnation of the majority of the human race is part of God's loving providence to make the fortunate saved ones appreciate their blessedness the more. Perhaps in an earlier age, when most of those with whom Christians came into contact were either fellow-Christians or were the sworn enemies of Christianity, such views were easier to accept. In modern South Africa, with the need to break down barriers between the races, where significant numbers of South Africans of Indian descent are Hindus or Moslems, and a proportion of South African black people are followers of primal religion, such views are part of the problem, not part of the solution.

South Africa is not the only country in the world where religious differences are part of the reason for oppression and violence. We cannot fail to take into account that it was Christians who carried out, or who at least condoned, the Holocaust, and that the inhumanity of Auschwitz was but the climax of many centuries of persecution of Jews by Christians. Rosemary Radford Ruether[103] suggests that antisemitism is built into the New Testament itself and into subsequent Christian tradition. It did not arise as an unfortunate deviation from true Christian ethics and teaching, but was an intrinsic part of the tradition, the almost inevitable result of Christian–Jewish rivalry. Christians believed that Jesus was the Messiah, Jews did not. Christians believed that Jesus was the revelation of all truth. The Jewish prophets, in Christian eyes, had not really been Jews but proto-Christians pointing to the truth of Jesus' claims. Jews who refused to recognize this or to acknowledge Jesus' messiahship were therefore believed to have been wilfully blind, setting up a deliberate falsehood in the place of Christian truth. It was therefore possible for Christians to marginalize them, see them as evil, and even liquidate them. The only way to avoid Christian antisemitism, in Ruether's view, is to excise from the New Testament and from Christian teaching all references to Jesus as

being the only truth, or the only Saviour. Hyam Maccoby makes
this point even more strongly:

> The remedy to antisemitism does not lie in cosmetic excisions of
> 'rejectionist' passages in the New Testament, nor in exhortations
> to recognize Judaism as an independent religion, much as these
> measures are to be welcomed. It lies in radical criticism of the
> central Christian myth of salvation, as a means of shifting guilt
> and responsibility.[104]

Religious arrogance is part of that from which we need to be
saved. This is more keenly part of our consciousness now. With
easier communication leading to a shrinking of the world, with the
post-colonial growth of religions other than Christianity in the
West, and with the rise of religious studies as a discipline distinct
from theology, we are more conscious of the richness and beauty of
other traditions, and the fact that saintly and heroic lives are not
confined to the Christian tradition. Orthodox christology has to be
able to show that it has taken this into account.

By no means all of those who defend the Chalcedonian definition
believe that non-Christians are damned or are without saving grace.
They certainly do not all, or even mostly, condone antisemitism or
intolerance towards other religions. It is arguable that Paul himself
with his reference to natural conscience in his letter to the Romans
was implying that the Hellenistic world had access before Christianity to God's grace – though Paul seems to have meant that natural
conscience was an agent of damnation, along with the Jewish law,
rather than of salvation, since no one, in Paul's view, is able to obey
conscience and all have sinned.[105]

Karl Rahner with his concept of anonymous Christianity[106]
argues that all religions contain 'elements of supernatural influence
by grace'. Their members are therefore already on the road to
salvation and can be regarded as anonymous Christians. Rahner has
been criticized for the tactlessness and arrogance of implying that,
for example, Moslems really worship Jesus without knowing it; but
of course this is going further than Rahner intended. He does not
say that such persons worship Christ. He is only extending the
Logos concept to say that the Word of God is already operative in
all creation outside the confines of official institutional Christianity.
Nevertheless I suspect that Rahner's argument carries within it
powerful criticism of orthodox christology if followed through
logically. For if the saving grace of God is operative in other
religions before the full Christian gospel is learnt; if members of

such religions can be *saved* by this grace, which Rahner seems to mean,[107] then there is no soteriological necessity for an incarnation. We may still argue that an incarnation is a fitting climax to this process of God's self-revelation, or an apt finishing touch, but it is not soteriologically necessary. Thus the cornerstone of Chalcedonian christology is removed.

Perhaps we may wish to cover our tracks and say that, although other religions have some saving power, Christianity has more; or perhaps we may say that although God's Word is inevitably present in all human life, only in Christianity is it possible to respond to God's word, since only in Christianity is sin forgiven. Other religions then prepare the way for Christianity but ultimately Christian conversion is still necessary for salvation. Then, however, we are still left with a morally questionable God who neglects to give some persons full grace or as good a chance as Christians for salvation for no other reason than that they have had the misfortune to be born into a non-Christian culture.

Amongst the defenders of a full incarnational christology, Hebblethwaite is commendably frank about this point. He concedes that:

> The most powerful argument against traditional incarnational Christology comes out of the encounter of religions; for it is very hard to do justice to the spirituality and religious worth of the great world religions and at the same time to maintain the divinity and hence finality of Christ.[108]

If Jesus is uniquely divine, then other religions are not of equal truth with Christianity, though Hebblethwaite regards himself as an inclusivist (i.e. the whole truth which the doctrine of incarnation represents includes some of the truths grasped in other religions) and not an exclusivist (i.e. there is no truth in other religions). He recognizes the moral problem of his position, but believes it to be necessary if the essential truth unique to Christianity is to be preserved.

Hebblethwaite may be right. If belief in the divinity of Jesus is necessary for salvation, then the moral problem of non-universalism just has to be accepted as mystery; but it is, nevertheless, a moral problem, and one of growing significance, particularly in South Africa.[109]

Rahner's anonymous Christianity has more to do with a kind of extended Logos doctrine than with the idea that the human Jesus, his life and his death, is of universal significance – though Rahner, of course, is not denying the latter. But how is the human Jesus significant for those who have never heard of him? Unless we have a very strong concept of human solidarity, so strong that we believe with some of the Eastern fathers that in some mystical way Jesus' life and death does recreate and change the whole human race, even though this does not know about him, or unless we argue for a vicarious atonement, that in his death Jesus paid for the sins of the whole world whether the world knows it or not, it is hard to see how he is of universal significance. Moule argues that in the eyes of the New Testament writers the death of Jesus has significance for all persons and for all time.[110] But without belief in a historical Adam and Eve and in Jesus as the new Adam, is a consequent strong belief in a corporate human personality possible? We may still believe in a weaker way in human solidarity, that is, in the influence that each person has upon others around. We may concede that in a shrinking world of instant news and television satellite pictures the interdependence of each human culture with others is stronger than before. But can we still believe that Jesus influenced even those who went before him, or whose culture is entirely removed from his historical influence? Surely we can believe this only in such an attenuated way as to make the concept of universal salvation in Jesus devoid of serious meaning. I believe we simply cannot share New Testament theology in this respect.

The issue here is not that of whether a Cantwell Smith-type of world theology is possible,[111] or whether Christianity and other world religions are all partial accounts of an overall truth that is greater than any of them. It would be difficult today to make the case that all religions are really saying the same thing in different ways or aiming at the same goal – that 'all roads lead to heaven'. It is a simpler issue. Traditional Christianity has claimed that we must believe that Jesus is God, for only then can his saving power be accounted for. If that is the case, then other religions which operate on lines quite different from Christianity are excluded from the fullness of salvation, which is morally unpalatable. We may say that those who do not know Christ, or are not able, through no fault of their own, to respond to Christ in this life, may still come to know him and be saved by him in the next life. This may be true – but removes the main concern of soteriological theory from this life to the next, and means that God still leaves most people unsaved in this life, which is the same moral problem. If other religions do have saving power distinct from a relationship with the person of Jesus, then we are let off the moral hook but caught on a new one.

Salvation in this view is possible without reference to the person of Jesus. In that case the basic Chalcedonian reason for claiming the two natures of Jesus is substantially weakened.

6. The concept of personality is a particularly perplexing one in modern times. What exactly is it about Jesus which is divine? It would be nonsense to say that Jesus had a divine yet physical body, for a physical body is a steadily changing agglomeration of cells which individually die and are replaced. To be ridiculous, what could it possibly mean to say that Jesus had a divine leg, or a divine oesophagus? The concept of incarnation is that the divine person *enters* a human body; the body is a vehicle for, a vessel of, divinity rather than divine in itself. The Apollinarian debate was about whether, in addition to entering a human body (which Apollinarius believed), the Logos also became incarnated in a human personality or soul (which Apollinarius did not believe).

Of course we may say with the Chalcedonian fathers that the person of Jesus cannot be divided up into parts, some parts human and some divine; but unless we have some concept of soul, or mind, or personality, which is distinct from the body, how can we talk about the divinity of Jesus at all? Austin Farrer comments:

> But the flesh is not the point of union; the divine action does not fuse with the throbbing of Jesus' pulses; it fuses with the movement of his mind.[112]

If those who hold that the mind is no more than the brain are right, if there is nothing other than the physical body, then a concept of incarnation will be very difficult, if not impossible, to defend. Morris argues that belief in a monistic human nature does not make belief in incarnation logically impossible, but nevertheless he does seem to think that a dualistic view is more congruous with that belief.[113]

We do not yet know that the mind-brain identity theorists are right. Theologians themselves are very divided. The respective articles on Soul in the *Dictionary of Christian Theology* and the *New Dictionary of Christian Theology*[114] illustrate this division very neatly. In the former volume, Alan Richardson prefers to say that belief in a soul is speculative and not required by the Bible. In the latter, Paul Badham argues strongly that the concept of a soul is very important for Christian belief. Whichever side we choose, the concept of soul is extremely difficult to pin down in any philosophically meaningful way, and is thus a problem for traditional views.

In fact, with Constantinople II and the doctrine of *enhypostasia*, the early church abandoned any idea that Jesus had a human personality, and taught that his human personality was the Logos. Thus O'Collins denies that Jesus was a human person at all:

> Jesus Christ was (and is) then a man, a human being, and a human individual, *but not* (his italics) a human person.[115]

Nevertheless he asserts that '. . . through his humanity Jesus Christ enjoyed his own rationality and freedom'.[116] There are considerable problems for me in understanding how *enhypostasia* differs from Apollinarianism, or how, if Jesus' human personality is the Logos, he can be humanly rational and free.

O'Collins insists that the person of the Logos entered human form. Jesus is not a human person, but the divine second person of the Trinity. This opens up the very complicated area of defining what is meant, in trinitarian doctrine, by God being three persons and one God. Tertullian's Latin *una substantia, tres personae* was translated by the Greek church, especially the Cappadocians, with great wariness. Basil was at pains to show that in his Greek terminology of one *ousia* and three *hypostases*, *hypostasis* did not denote a 'person' as a human individual. That need not concern us now. The point is that if the doctrine of *enhypostasia* is held, then Jesus' personality means something very different from a human personality. Human personality, as we have already remarked, grows from experience, from contact with others, from exercising free choice where there is a real possibility of choosing incorrectly and having to overcome the consequences of that. If none of this is true for Jesus (which it cannot be if his personality means the same thing as the Logos), then it is very difficult to see how Jesus' humanity consists of any more than being temporarily encased in a human body. Since our bodies and our personality or soul (or whatever we believe makes us a human person) are in any case interdependent and form a psychosomatic whole, so that a bodily illness affects our personality, personality for us has a constantly changing quality, even though there may be a certain basic consistency. Can we say that the Logos is constantly changing? None of these are new issues, as the debate over Apollinarianism shows; but modern behaviourist psychology sharpens the issue for us considerably.

7. Traditional christology requires us to say that God acted in Jesus in a unique way: that the actions of Jesus were the actions of God. Liberal Christians sometimes want to state this less strongly,

and to say that Jesus was human rather than divine, but was uniquely obedient to God, so that God was able to act through him uniquely.[117] Yet the whole concept of God acting through humans is in itself an extremely problematic one which has not yet really been resolved. A debate in *Religious Studies* and *Theology*[118] between Maurice Wiles, Brian Hebblethwaite and David Galilee highlighted the problem, and although Austin Farrer is invoked as an answer, I am not convinced that Farrer takes us much further. The problem lies in differentiating between God's actions and human actions. How can there be two agencies responsible for a single action? Where does human action stop and God's action begin? It is true that Farrer makes a valuable contribution to this debate about double agency in one of his typical arguments between himself and an imaginary partner where (again typically), he shows his inventive genius by arriving, apparently independently, at much the same point as process theology. It is never easy, as Wiles remarks, to pin down exactly what Farrer means: but in essence it appears to be that God does not act in this world except as the mind of the world: he enters the world's constituents '. . . by prior causality, willing them into existence and the activity they exercise'.[119] Having created them, he leaves them to make their own actions.

> His concern for his creatures is for them to be themselves, or more than themselves; not for them to act as pawns in some specifically supernatural game which any divine hand is bound to play.[120]

'Double agency' is therefore meant by Farrer only in a very reduced sense. God initiates by constantly willing the world's constituents into being. God does not act in the world. 'The world is so made as to run itself.'[121] God's actions are to create, and constantly to confront the world with his will and purposes. Farrer is no pantheist. The fact that the voice of God is met with only in what he has made does not mean that everything we meet is the voice of God. Concerning the story of Saul consulting the Witch of Endor, Farrer says:

> If God is a living will and a heart of love directly concerned for us, why should we look for him, or why listen for him, in the remote and dubious margins of our experience. It is folly . . . to look away from the point where God's will touches us in our present

existence . . . The will of God is everywhere present: it is experienced by being obeyed.[122]

Farrer means that what God does is to call us to act in obedience to his will: and that the evidence of God's act of willing and calling can best be seen in the lives of Jesus and of the saints. Even in the life of Jesus, however, what we perceive is his obedience to God's call. God does not, on this account, so it seems to me, act in Jesus in any way differently from how he acts in us. I suspect that Farrer and Wiles are saying very much the same thing.

Wiles gives extended attention to the problem of God's action in the world.[123] He argues that for a number of reasons – the regularity and growing explicability of the physical world where God as *deus ex machina* is less and less needed; more importantly the fact that blessing and disaster are both found in that world so that if God is seen to be directly involved in blessing it is hard to deny his action in bane – it makes more sense to say that God does not actively intervene in the world.

This is not, Wiles believes, the same as Deism. God is not withdrawn from the world. Nor is Wiles returning to a neo-Platonic view of an immutable God who is removed from the universe. Much as Farrer argued, Wiles believes that God is present at every level in every action in the world, in the sense that he has created all things and holds them in being; he is the ongoing source of their energy and life. Each creature in the universe is nevertheless free, within its own created nature, to make its own choices. If this applies at a sub-human level, it applies even more at a human level. Wiles puts a '. . . strong emphasis on the radical degree of freedom with which I believe the human creation to have been endowed'.[124]

God's action in the world is constant. It is one of creation and of establishing the overall purpose for creation. Wiles rejects the idea of any *special* action of God, either in miracles of nature, healing miracles, or special grace to certain individuals. I would argue that he is right. God's purposes are surely stable and constant, and his love equally disposed. Why would he intervene with special miracles in some cases and not in all? And if he intervened in all cases, they would no longer be miracles, exceptions to the rule. If God is active in some historical acts, for example in leading the people of Israel out of Egypt, he must be equally active in all historical events, in which case the exile is his work too. Old Testament Jews were able to say of the exile that it was indeed God's action, the consequence of their own sin, and rationalize it in that way; but what then of God's involvement in the Holocaust, surely beyond rationalization. We may explain that the Holocaust is the result of human free will, and thus indirectly attributable to God who made us with that freedom. We surely cannot say, as the Old Testament Jews were able of the exile, that God wished or intended the Holocaust or was directly involved in bringing it about. If God is seen to have taken what we might call direct action in some cases, he must either act equally in all, or be held accountable for his lack of action. God then becomes morally blameworthy, unless we take refuge in mystery and say that his apparent immorality is only attributable to our imperfect understanding, which must blunt our own moral sensibility. Otherwise we must say, with Wiles, that God's actions are those of creation and calling, but that beyond that he does not intervene or overthrow the free choices of his creatures.

In what way, then, can God be said to have acted in Jesus differently from how he acts in all humans? The New Testament understands Jesus as the culmination of God's actions both in history and in personal individuals. The virgin birth and the resurrection certainly suggest the special action of God. However, Wiles makes the familiar but true observation that the New Testament narrative about Jesus is best understood as retrospective perception of Jesus' significance for the church community rather than as an historical account in the way modern history would be written. It seems to me that the objections raised above about the special action of God in history also apply to special action of God in Jesus, although this is going beyond Wiles' point. If God acted in a unique and special way in Jesus, why did he wait so long? And why did he not act in other histories and cultures?

It is not clear to me in what sense Wiles believes in the resurrection, whether as objective physical event or an event in the subjective awareness of the disciples. Nor in *God's Action in the World* does Wiles trace out the implications of that book for a doctrine of incarnation. However the logical problems of believing in God's special, one-off action in the world seem to me to apply as strongly to belief in the Incarnation as a distinctive, different action by God in Jesus which God does not will to do in every other person. That does not mean that Jesus is not unique. We may well argue that in his response and whole-hearted obedience to God Jesus is unique, that he is thus a unique saviour who makes it possible for God to act uniquely in him as God would *like* to act in every person.

Wiles goes on to show how a reduced belief in God's action in the world is not incompatible with a continuing practice of prayer, worship and sacraments. Indeed one could make a case for saying that it strengthens these practices, as channels to the underlying and constant creation and calling of God rather than as semi-magical purveyors of special miracles. However, that is beside our present point.

By way of contrast with Wiles, Brian Hebblethwaite suggests that:

> Most theologians would now affirm that, at least in his relation to the world, God is a God who acts, and that the story of God's dealings with his people constitutes an unfolding and indeed unfinished history . . . The influence of Platonism is on the wane.[125]

This is an important point, and one to which I shall return in later chapters. It helps to clarify what Wiles is *not* saying. Hebblethwaite is surely right; in a world which is increasingly aware of suffering it is intolerable to believe in the old classic way in an immutable, impassible God who is not involved except as distant transcendent first cause and prime mover in his world. Wiles is not arguing that God is not active and present in the world, but that God does not act in special, different ways at some points or in some persons in history. Wiles's case rests not on Platonic concepts of the immutability of God, but on the more telling grounds of divine consistency of justice, fairness and constancy of love. I think it is hard to refute.

The question, then, for a traditional view of the Incarnation is how the actions of Jesus can be spoken of as divine actions. If Jesus is both God and man, how far are his actions divine and how far human? Does it add anything to our understanding of Jesus to say that when he spoke words of forgiveness he spoke not just on God's behalf, just as God's spokesman, but with the voice of God himself? When he urged his followers to enter the Kingdom of God, did he invite them as spokesman for God, or as God himself? When he stilled the winds and waters (granting the truth of the nature miracles for the moment) did he still them as the Creator of his universe, or as the servant of God speaking with the confidence that the Creator would hear and heed? Whatever traditional Christianity may say about the *communicatio idiomatum* (the interrelation of human and divine in Jesus, so that his actions can be described as being both divine and human in one breath), does such language really add very much to our interpretation and understanding of the events? Is there a significant difference between speaking as one who himself loves and serves God and assuring the woman taken in adultery that she is not condemned by the God who is her 'Abba', and speaking as God to the woman with the same assurance?

Perhaps we shall have recourse to the idea of God confronting the world with his will and purposes through a human Jesus acting as God's spokesman or representative. Perhaps Jesus' unique obedience made it possible for God to speak to the world as never before. This might be the liberal answer. For liberal Christians who want to say that Jesus is human rather than divine, but a human person who is a vehicle for God's actions, there is another problem. How can God be thought of as acting through the human person Jesus? If special divine action is ruled out, as I have supported Wiles in saying, then all that is meant by such language about Jesus is that, as a human person, he responded in a unique way to the underlying grace of God and the ever-present call of God, equally available to us but to which we respond and obey to a much lesser degree. The actions of Jesus would be his own actions, in obedience to God, certainly, made possible by the ever-present grace of God and in this sense the actions of a son of God, but nonetheless his actions and not God's. This is much less than liberal Christians usually wish to say. Sympathetic Jews, Moslems, and Hindus could probably accept such a formulation without much of a problem. But if special divine action is ruled out, what other formulation would be possible? And if special divine action is not ruled out, we are left with the problems which Wiles has raised.

There is, of course, the refuge of mystery, a refuge to which we might still need to have recourse if the basic Chalcedonian assumption – no full incarnation, no salvation – is found to be true.

8. Cupitt insists that the ideal modern view of humanness is of autonomous persons, choosing for ourselves what in the light of our reason seems to us to be the most appropriate values and actions, and not forced by outside persons, human or divine. He argues that Jesus himself, if he is truly human, must have had the same freedom: freedom to err and indeed freedom even to sin.[126] Not to have this freedom is to be less than fully human. For Jesus to avoid sin because he is by divine nature unable to sin is to reduce the human praiseworthiness of his goodness: but then, if he is free to sin, how can we talk in the traditional way of his being God?

To return for a moment to the pre-Chalcedonian debate, we have seen that for the Alexandrians the humanness of Jesus was of a very reduced kind. Following the Platonic tendency to stress genus or class more than the individual, they had little idea of Jesus as an individual, decision-making human being. The Antiochenes laid more stress on the individual humanness of Jesus – but with the two-sons theory of Diodore lurking in the background. Like Cyril, we cannot accept Diodore's thesis; but with a modern understanding of the value and importance of the individual we cannot follow the Alexandrian route either. Our concept of humanness is fuller than, or at least different from, the Alexandrian one. We see individuality, individual choice and responsibility as being a strength and a virtue. To be fully and ideally human Jesus must possess these qualities, with the consequent difficulty in calling him divine also. His actions must be human actions, not God's actions through him – but then how can he be divine?

When faced with the question 'Can God will what is evil or illogical, and if not, is this then a limitation on God's freedom and power?', Thomas Aquinas replied that for God to do what is less than morally or logically perfect would itself be a limitation of his nature, so that the problem is a false problem; if God did what is evil, that would constitute a limitation of God.

We might argue, then, that Jesus, divine and human, might humanly have chosen sin but in his divinity could not do so since this would again imply imperfection. For the Chalcedonians this did not entail a serious problem, for a true, perfect human being equally would not sin, so that there was no logical problem involved in saying that Jesus, God and man, was fully and perfectly human and could not sin. He could endure temptation; he could know the drives of hunger, thirst and fear; but it was impossible for him to have succumbed to that temptation.

The issue is not so easy for us. To be human, to know humanly, is to know by the exercise of choice and by learning from experience. We have no eternal Platonic 'ideal' of humanness. There was no past human perfection. The experience on which we base our knowledge will certainly stretch beyond our own experience to include the experience of our predecessors and our community, but this will not give us a sufficient basis to make a perfect choice. We do not know what is sinful until we learn it from the community and from our own experience. The community's view of what is sinful will always be less than perfect. Perfect moral choice is not a meaningful human possibility. The exercise of autonomous moral choice, and the obligation to live through the consequence, is what constitutes the human challenge; but how can this be ascribed to a divine person if we wish 'divine' to retain any meaning? The process theology concept of a limited, growing deity might provide some refuge, but this would be much less than Chalcedon meant, and

would consequently have been seen by Chalcedon as soteriologically inadequate – a criticism which is levelled against the process
concept of God anyway.

In a subsequent chapter I shall refer to Morris, who believes that
his two-minds approach allows for this problem. In his human mind
Jesus may have had to learn, cognitively, what constitutes 'goodness'. He may have faced temptation and in his human mind not
have known that he was incapable of sin. Thus sin would have been
an 'epistemic' but not an ontological, actual possibility for him. The
battle against sin would have been just as real, for he would not have
known, humanly, that he would win the battle. Morris offers some
analogies to illustrate the point.[127] In his divine mind, we may say,
Jesus knew perfectly and ominisciently. In his human mind his
knowledge is humanly limited, including knowledge of his own
sinlessness.

The problem with Morris' approach is that it drives a wedge
between Jesus' divine and human minds, which surely makes the
Incarnation a much lesser identification of God and human in Jesus.
I discuss the point below.[128] When all these problems are considered along with the problems of understanding God as acting in the
world in any special way at all, as discussed in the previous section,
we see that Cupitt has raised a fairly weighty objection.

9. Although we shall deal with it fully below, I mention another
modern issue here, which is that of suffering. We feel keenly aware
of the existence of suffering, hunger, oppression, in our world, or if
we do not feel keenly aware we know that we ought to. Modern
media keep the world's tragedies before us. The rise of liberation
theology is a recognition that the issue is of theological importance.
The majority of Christians (if not the majority of theologians) in the
world today are in the suffering, Third-World part of humanity.

Suffering is not new. Many of the early Christians were as poor
and as vulnerable as Third-World Christians now. The Old
Testament is full of assurance that God cares for the oppressed and
the suffering, and intervenes in history on their behalf. The
intervention of God is itself a problematical concept, as we have
already seen, a matter to which we will give more attention later.
Yet if God does not intervene to end the suffering, it becomes
increasingly difficult to believe in him. Theodicy, that is, reconciling
belief in a God of love with the existence and extent of suffering, has
never been more difficult than in our post-Holocaust world. Since
the mediaeval and Reformation church, the problem for theology
has shifted from justifying humans before an accusing God to

justifying God before an accusing humanity. Is it conceivable that a loving God could have permitted Auschwitz? Nowhere is this problem more acute than in South Africa.

> Just as the contemporary theological debate on suffering has been sparked off by events such as the Holocaust and Hiroshima, so within our own context [i.e. the South African one], theological reflection on suffering is called for by the reality of apartheid, and should be grounded in it.[129]

God seems to have no power to stop or prevent evil which is on a scale too great to be endured. In any discussion of the saving work of Jesus, we cannot overlook the stark experience of black South African people. John de Gruchy reports the words of a forlorn black woman taken by force to live in a barren 'homeland'.

> My man has gone and died, as have my daughters. They took my land away. The Lord has also gone, yes, I suppose he has also gone.[130]

Part of the message of the New Testament is that Jesus himself suffered. It seems to have been a particularly strong stress in Mark's Gospel. Not for nothing has that Gospel been called a passion story with a long introduction. In a situation where Christianity had begun to be persecuted, it was important to know that Jesus himself had been persecuted.

In one way a full incarnational view of Jesus strengthens the message that God cares about suffering, for in this view the Son of God himself suffered. In due course, however, the church would have to address the problem of how God can be said to suffer. The problem became more acute once the classic concept of theism had become entrenched, with its stress on the incorporeality and the aseity, the utter independence of God. If God is perfect, God cannot be vulnerable. Patripassianism was rejected, i.e. the idea that if Jesus was identical with the Father, then in Jesus' sufferings on the cross the Father suffers. In that case we must say that not the Father, but the Son, the Logos, who is God, suffers. But if the Father cannot suffer because he is God, then how can the Son, who is equally God, suffer? Thus the early church had to say that Jesus suffers in his human, not his divine, capacity – driving a wedge between the two natures of Jesus in a somewhat Nestorian manner.

It is true that for this reason some more modern concepts of God, for example process theology, argue that God can suffer, and is vulnerable. Bonhoeffer said that God becomes weak and powerless in the world, and thus is the only true help.[131] Others, for example Jürgen Moltmann and the South African theologian John de Gruchy, have also argued from other perspectives for a God who suffers. Karl Rahner has suggested that God, while immutable in himself, becomes mutable in another, and that what happens to Jesus is also God's history.[132] We may take it that mutability implies vulnerability. Whether a vulnerable God is a very satisfactory concept of God is a whole debate in itself. I am only arguing that if we take human Third-World suffering seriously, then the sufferings of Jesus are an important link between Jesus and the suffering world, but the question of *how* Jesus' human sufferings also link God with the suffering world has not yet been satisfactorily answered. Here again we are faced with a mystery which we must show to be a necessary mystery if we are to be properly 'economic' in our christology. The concept of a vulnerable God, a God who becomes mutable *in alio*, is perhaps an unnecessarily complicated concept unless we can show that if Jesus be not divine, there is no salvation.

These, then, are some of the factors of our modern consciousness which make it imperative that the Chalcedonian Definition be at least re-evaluated, as we ask how it can make sense to us in our modern culture. Chalcedon conceded the difficulty, but insisted that unless Jesus is fully divine and fully human, we cannot be saved. We are more acutely aware, given our modern understanding, of the difficulty. Although we have touched upon the concept of salvation, we shall have to examine it more fully in the following pages. We shall discover that in our modern situation even the concept of salvation has changed. To add to our difficulties, we do not have a *philosophia perennis* as in earlier times. There is no agreed single philosophical world-view which holds sway. Rahner makes it clear that we live in a world of philosophical pluralism.[133]

This is not a new situation for the christological debate. I have suggested that the New Testament church itself had many different philosophies and christological views. H. E. W. Turner suggests that the use of Greek philosophy meant the loss of some of the biblical flexibility of outlook, but the gain of a more stable and coherent framework.[134] In our own time, the Greek framework no longer fits the whole spectrum of our experience, and we are pushed into flexibility again. Whether this is a forward or a backward push is a matter of perspective. Rahner welcomes modern pluralism as a stage of necessary confusion and uncertainty on the way towards a fuller apprehension of the whole reality in a better, more adequate world view.[135] However, the emergence of that comprehensive philosophy lies in the future, and is not presently to hand. The same applies, as Sutherland says, to an emergence of an agreed reconstruction of the historical Jesus. Biblical scholars as well as philosophical theologians are subject to uncertainties and confusions as well. Nonetheless, Sutherland asks, 'Can and need the eternal significance of faith wait on the results of historical enquiry which can at best be approximate and revisable in principle?'[136]

We have to try to develop an understanding of Jesus and his salvation in a way that fits our present incomplete and unsatisfactory philosophical and biblical understanding. Our revised christology may in the end prove to need substantial revision itself. We may discover that the traditional views which we have left on the back burner, which we have temporarily put aside as being currently unhelpful, are in fact true and relevant after all. In the meantime, we have to reconstruct a christology which is as coherent and as consistent with our current experience as possible.

5

Problems with Abandoning Chalcedon

I have suggested above that all the problems posed for modern people in believing the full Chalcedonian Definition of the nature of Jesus do not mean that we have proved that the traditional doctrine is wrong, but only that it is possibly not the best way of interpreting our own experience. If it can be shown that our experience demands such a belief, then it is not logically incoherent to say that the belief, although it transcends our present understanding and is mysterious to us, is true.

Alister McGrath remarks that the liberal theologians who turn away from belief in the literal divinity of Jesus do so because they are conditioned by post-Enlightenment philosophy into assuming that traditional belief is incoherent.

> Modern Christian theology has been oppressed by the spirit of the eighteenth-century Enlightenment, on occasion even giving the impression of being a willing prisoner.[137]

McGrath regrets that the old idea of *fides quaerens intellectum*, 'I believe so that I may understand', has given way to a spirit of 'unless I understand I will not believe'.

McGrath is one amongst a number of theologians who argue that all rational systems have certain foundations, or what Polanyi calls a 'fiduciary framework'.[138] The logical system is then built on that framework, and as a system must satisfy the demands of logic; but the foundations themselves are not provable or disprovable on rational grounds.

One could therefore argue that the sort of logical problems with

the traditional doctrine of the Incarnation which were outlined in
the previous section are only problems if one takes the sort of stance
which post-Enlightenment critics of traditional doctrine adopt; i.e.
that knowledge is limited to that for which we have empirical evidence, etc. One could then go on to argue, as McGrath does, that
this post-Enlightenment stance is itself a fiduciary framework, not a
self-evident or necessary truth. One could argue that belief in the
Incarnation is something like Plantinga's belief in God: a 'properly
basic' belief which does not require rational proof or demonstra-
tion.[139]

However, I believe that to argue in this way is to miss the point of
the problems in the last section. I do not suggest that the traditional
doctrine of the Incarnation is impossible to reconcile with logic, but
only that it does not provide as close a fit with modern experience,
as good an interpretation of contemporary knowledge, as previ-
ously. It is not as useful as it once was. Now of course 'useful' does
not mean 'true', nor 'non-useful' mean 'untrue'. But the Christian
claim is surely not only that Christian faith is true, or consistent with
a sufficiently sophisticated logic (it is not merely a metaphysic), but
that it is true *and* useful. If traditional doctrines no longer prove
helpful, that does not mean in strict logic that they are no longer
true, but it may mean that they are no longer salvific. Such a
situation must surely mean that we need to re-examine both the
truth and the necessity of the old doctrinal formulations.

I think the same objections can be raised about the very
sophisticated work of T. V. Morris, collected together in his *The
Logic of God Incarnate*. He deals with three possible attacks on the
doctrine of the Incarnation: that the doctrine is incoherent in
making the identity statement 'Jesus is identical with the Son of
God'; that the vastness of the cosmos makes the doctrine cosmically
incongruent; and that if Jesus is truly human and fully human there
can then be no evidence of incarnation since if Jesus is different
from us he would not be fully human. Morris also deals with how the
doctrine relates to the traditional doctrine of the Trinity. He
believes that the doctrine of the Incarnation along Chalcedonian
lines can be shown to be logical and coherent and meaningful.

Morris does not compromise by taking any easy ways out in
considering whether the doctrine of the Incarnation is incoherent.
He refuses to take a Kierkegaardian line that theology need not
meet logical requirements, that human philosophy is irrelevant to
our knowledge of God. He refuses to say that the strict requirements for identity-statements (the principle of indiscernibility of

identicals) do not apply to Jesus Christ because he is *sui generis*. He chooses not to take a kenotic line or to water down the apparently irreconcilable divine qualities, so far as incarnation in human nature is concerned, as immutability, omniscience or omnipotence.

> So it seems clear that a defender of the orthodox doctrine of the Incarnation ought not to respond to the contemporary challenge based on the indiscernibility principle by either devaluing the status of human logic, rejecting the problem outright, or revising it in such a way as to square with what seem to be essential divine-human property differences. The best response to the challenge will consist in meeting it head on in acknowledging the governance of the traditional indiscernibility principle over identity statements and arguing that, contrary to what has been alleged, the incarnational identity [i.e. Jesus is God the Son] satisfies the requirements.[140]

By the 'principles of the indiscernibility of the identicals' Morris means that if object 'x' is identical with object 'y', then every property possessed by 'x' is possessed by 'y' and vice versa. On the face of it, this principle means that it should be extremely difficult to show how Jesus of Nazareth, possessing human properties, can be identical with God the Son. Again, Morris uncompromisingly says that the doctrine of the Incarnation

> . . . is not true unless Jesus had all and only the properties of . . . the individual referred to in Christian theology as God the Son.[141]

He claims that a 'significant number' of contemporary theologians have held this identity-statement to be not only false, i.e. untrue in fact, but impossible, incoherent, unintelligible; and he sets out to show that the doctrine is no such thing. He does this by making some simple, perfectly legitimate, distinctions between such things as common properties and essential properties. For example, it is common for humans to have lived at some time on the earth, but not necessarily essential to their humanity if space travel becomes a reality. It is common to humans to have a beginning in time, and to die, and thus to be what would classically be known as 'contingent', but it is not logically imperative to say that contingency is then essential to what it means to be human. Jesus then could be said to be human and yet not contingent. Morris draws a distinction, too, between 'merely human' and 'fully human'. A mere human is sinful, but must a full human then be sinful too? Mere humanity may be common, may in fact apply to everybody except Jesus, but 'mereness', because common, is not therefore essential to being human.

Morris takes what he calls an Anselmian view of God. God is therefore in his view omniscient and omnipotent. God is also essentially immutable. How then can Jesus be God the Son, and therefore omnipotent, etc., and yet also possess a truly human mind, without any change in the qualities of omniscience? Although Morris believes that logical coherence *could* be shown for a kenotic approach, that is to say, an approach which says that in the Incarnation God the Son voluntarily divested himself of his omniscience and omnipotence, he does not favour this, since it would weaken too far what he regards as another essential quality of God, i.e. his immutability. Thus in his view God (and therefore God the Son) unchangeably possesses all the kind-essential attributes of his deity, which include all the 'omni-' qualities. God can *add* further attributes, provided these are not contradictory to the existing attributes (thus Morris is not an absolute immutabilist), but God cannot *lose* them.

In the Incarnation, therefore, Jesus did not lose any of his divine attributes, according to Morris, but he added to them a human mind. In Jesus there are two ranges of consciousness: eternal, omniscient, intuitive; and temporal, limited and developing. The first set of qualities includes the second. Thus in his human mind Jesus grows, learns, needs teaching, is limited to his historical and cultural viewpoint. But all of what he knows in his human mind is included in his divine mind. There is no logical contradiction.

Morris offers various analogies to show that his two-minds theory is not inconceivable.

> But can we really understand what it is to attribute two minds, or two ranges of consciousness, to one person?[142]

He reminds us that we cannot know what it is to be God, or for God to possess two minds – a retreat into mystery, but not illogical for all that. He offers the analogy of dream consciousness in which I am a participant in the action of a dream story but simultaneously know that I am the dreamer. He reminds us that modern psychology claims that there are various strata of the mind, e.g. subconscious and conscious, operating simultaneously. He refers to occasional instances of multiple personality. All analogies, of course, have their weaknesses: we might object to Morris that a dream world is not a real world, while incarnation requires that Jesus be really human; that psychologists regard states of divided consciousness as pathological rather than ideal.

Morris says:

> If it is defensible, which I think it is, the two minds view along with the distinctions [between common and essential qualities, between mere and full humanity] . . . gives us all we need for philosophically explicating the orthodox doctrine of the Incarnation and defending it against all forms of the contemporary incoherence challenge.[143]

Morris's two-minds theory as I have suggested in the previous subsection, also enables him to deal with the problems of cosmological insignificance and of how Jesus can be really tempted.

This summary of Morris' closely packed arguments does not do justice to the detail and care of his work. I think that in fact he does show that the traditional doctrine of the Incarnation is neither antilogical nor entirely incoherent. The Chalcedonian fathers would not easily have recognized his version of the doctrine. His two-minds theory sounds a little like the two-sons theory which Cyril hated – though of course it is nothing of the kind, since Morris is clear that the human mind of Jesus is subsumed within the divine mind. But then the two consciousnesses of Jesus (the divine consciousness including the human so that he simultaneously knows all and does not know, simultaneously is able to do all things, knows that he is so able, and yet is humanly unaware of his divine omnipotence) makes of Jesus a person very different from ourselves. It is true that I may have a subconscious awareness of abilities in myself of which I am not consciously aware; but then I am not able to harness those abilities except vestigially. They are potential rather than actual. Jesus' divine attributes must surely be known to his divine consciousness, which cannot be a mere subconscious. His divine attributes cannot be potential and not actual – unless we go back to Vincent Taylor's version of kenoticism. Morris can argue in logic that this does not mean that Jesus is not human; he is fully human where we are merely human. If, however, Jesus does not share our 'mere' humanity, if in his human helplessness and weakness he is simultaneously and (divinely speaking) consciously, all powerful and all mighty, then does he share our condition? 'What is unassumed is unhealed', said the Cappadocians.

This is the chief difference between Morris and the theologians whom he criticizes. Morris, as a philosopher, is concerned with issues of coherence, meaning and logic. Theologians have to take that into account, but are also concerned, perhaps primarily concerned, with issues of helpfulness and relevance. I do not think that Morris is correct in saying that most contemporary theologians who are critical of the traditional doctrine of the Incarnation claim that the doctrine is 'impossible, self-contradictory, incoherent, absurd, and even unintelligible', although Don Cupitt does so. The real issue is not that the doctrine cannot be rendered coherent or logical, but that it is not relevant to the human situation.

From a philosophical point of view, relevance is no guarantee of truth. I am aware of the danger that a socially relevant religion is relevant only to its own time and has a built-in obsolescence. I have argued above that truths which once seemed very helpful and relevant may return to be helpful and relevant once more.[144] Christianity claims, however, to be not only true, but to be of saving truth, and saving truth does require a high degree of social relevance, to humans both individually and collectively. That is not to deny that we may be blind to what is truly of relevance to us. Social relevance does not mean merely what is commonly perceived to be socially relevant. Nor does it mean we are not concerned with what is universally and always true. It is a question, for Christianity, of trying to do both; to look for eternal verities, but also to say how these truths are evidence of God's love for us now.

There may be a certain irony in the spectacle of theologians trying to reinterpret the person and work of Jesus in ways which do not offend post-Enlightenment susceptibilities while some philosophers like Gadamer and Polanyi are saying that Enlightenment views are themselves outdated. It might seem that the church is, as so often, adapting too late to issues that are already *passé*. This criticism is not, however, entirely true. Modern critics of the doctrine of the Incarnation, those who wish to reinterpret it, are not always motivated by outdated philosophical demands for verifiability and for empiricism so much as by the conviction that the doctrine is no longer of *saving* truth. This is particularly evident in the work of Maurice Wiles.

In *The Logic of God Incarnate* Morris evidences no interest in issues of salvation. As a philosopher he is justified in that omission. He shows that the traditional doctrine can be defended against charges of incoherence or nonsense. If the doctrine is still needed to make sense of Christian claims that the person and work of Jesus are of saving significance, then Morris' work would be of great importance. However, since the doctrine grew out of soteriology, the soteriology must be prior and we must ask not only 'Is the doctrine logical?' but 'Is it the best explanation for what we experience as salvation in Jesus?' This is the question I shall try to address in a later part of this book.

It is not, then, true that all liberal christology is influenced only by sceptical rationalism, though that may sometimes be the case. It is concerned to discover and communicate the meaning not only of the Incarnation but of salvation. It is also influenced by modern biblical criticism – itself to some extent the product of sceptical rationalism, to be sure, but not entirely so. Some of the fruits of the labours of biblical critics are now widely accepted. McGrath and Hebblethwaite are not urging us to return to precritical fundamentalism. The distance between the historical Jesus and the Jesus of the evangelists is also a reason, quite apart from philosophy, for needing to reconsider a pre-critical christology.

There is little mileage to be gained by restricting religious belief to what can be proved on rational grounds to be unquestionably true. Since with religion we are dealing with ultimate 'metatruths', we must grant that the foundations for our theology may be metalogical. Our belief-systems need to be consistent with experience as well as with historical evidence and logic, and experience may transcend these latter criteria.

Hebblethwaite must therefore be taken seriously when he says that a liberal christology, while it may appear more logical, will cause us to lose much that is of real value in our Christian experience. He lists a number of these losses.

If Jesus is not truly God, then our knowledge of God is greatly lessened and our relationship with God made more distant.

> The moral and religious value of the Incarnation lies in the greatly increased potential for human knowledge of God and personal union with God introduced by God's own presence and acts in human form [i.e. in Jesus], this side of the gap between Creator and creature.[145]

Hebblethwaite concedes that in other religions people may come to know God, and to be in a close personal relationship with God through mysticism, but to a lesser degree than a much more direct, face-to-face way of personal encounter with God in Jesus.

If Jesus is not God, we cannot have a belief in a Trinity, a belief which enables us to see God in 'richer relational terms',[146] perceiving God as love in himself. If God is love, there must be a Trinity, or at least Binity, within the Godhead – unless we say that

God is love because he loves his creation which makes the creation eternally necessary to God, which is a denial of Godhead.

It can be seen that Hebblethwaite is quite influenced here by Leonard Hodgson[147] and his relational analogy of the Trinity, and perhaps by the Greek fathers, rather than by the more monistic trinitology of Augustine. Hebblethwaite acknowledges that belief in the Trinity did not historically come about because people recognized the necessity of love within the Godhead. Trinitology was a consequence of believing that Jesus was divine, rather than a cause. In retrospect, however, he believes, we can now see that without trinitarian belief, which requires that Jesus be divine, our concept of love within the Godhead would be damaged.

As an extension of belief in the Trinity, Christians are enabled to see themselves in their worship and sacraments as being caught up into the trinitarian love-relationship themselves, so that they become part of the Son's self-offering to the Father.[148] They are enabled to see themselves as part of Christ's body in a Pauline way,[149] enabled with Jesus to call God 'Abba', Father. If Jesus is not God, 'we no longer have a living saviour, by incorporation into whose body we too can say Abba, Father'.[150] A full trinitarian belief enables us to see that our response to God was not purely our response, but is God's own response in us to his own initiative.[151]

Unless Jesus is God, we can only say that God suffers with us in our sufferings in a very reduced way:

> This whole dimension of the Christian doctrine of the Incarnation, its recognition of the costly nature of God's forgiving love, and its perception that only a suffering God is morally credible, is lost if God's involvement is reduced to a matter of 'awareness' and 'sympathy'.[152]

This concept of God sharing our suffering and our humiliation with us is carried further by Hebblethwaite in his embracing of kenoticism, which I have already touched on.[153] It is central to the soteriology of Jürgen Moltmann, and will be considered under that heading later in this book.[154]

The traditional doctrine of the Incarnation has considerable ethical implications. That God became human gives a value and importance to human life that makes a great difference in an often impersonal world. It may have considerable political implications in struggles against capitalism, or régimes like South Africa that devalue human life. That God took on himself a human body means that the physical and material universe is given its proper, positive, non-Manichean place in the scheme of things. That God emptied himself and suffered with us on the cross underlines the central values of self-sacrifice and of service.[155]

We have already noted that Hebblethwaite joins others in pointing out that if Jesus is not divine it is more difficult to see why or how Jesus is central to human salvation, and that liberal assumptions that a human Jesus is still of universal human significance are difficult to sustain.[156] If liberals are right in ascribing to Jesus a unique closeness to God or harmony with God, then surely, says Hebblethwaite, a more consistent conclusion would be that Jesus is not only human but that 'his human life was lived out of a centre in God',[157] and that within his humanity God himself lives in a unique way.

Keith Ward[158] offers some criticism of these points, and although Hebblethwaite responds to these criticisms,[159] I do not think he meets Ward's objections. I incorporate some of Ward's criticisms in my own remarks.

There seems to be validity in Hebblethwaite's observations that much richness would be lost if traditional incarnational theology were to be abandoned, and that the concept of Jesus and of salvation offered by the liberal christologists is thin by comparison. However, we have to ask ourselves whether Hebblethwaite's construction of the rich concept of God about to be lost, is based on sufficiently firm foundations. As Ward points out, we do not in fact have a face-to-face relationship with the human Jesus upon which to build our understanding of an otherwise shadowy and transcendent God. The first disciples may have had this relationship: we do not. We may be said to have a relationship with the risen Jesus, or with Jesus-in-the-church, but this Jesus is as far removed from our immediate perception as is God himself. This Jesus is also transcendent, and not part of our concrete sense-experience. If it be said that although we do not ourselves have a face-to-face relationship with Jesus, we read about and thus share in that relationship as described in the New Testament, we come up against the problem of the reconstruction of the historical Jesus. This is not to say that no such reconstruction is possible in even the smallest degree, but the knowledge which we gain from this encounter at second hand with Jesus is not as direct as Hebblethwaite would have us believe.

What is more, our concept of God is not very different from that of other monotheistic religions. Islam, and particularly Judaism, also believes in a personal God who is a God of love and compassion, without this knowledge of God being mediated to them through Jesus (or only very indirectly, perhaps, in the case of Islam). In fact, therefore, Hebblethwaite's construction of a knowledge of God based on a face-to-face relationship with Jesus and leading to a concept of God much deeper and more intimate than in any other religions, proves not to mean so much in reality.

Again, Hebblethwaite's point that if Jesus is not God we cannot say that God is at one with us in our sufferings is not as powerful as it might at first seem. Ward comments that God being somehow involved in Jesus' sufferings is of no great help to the rest of us. God, if he loves us, must equally be involved in all of our suffering. We might say that although God does suffer with Jesus' sufferings, he suffers too with ours, so that the uniqueness of Jesus is not in the degree to which God identifies with him, but in the degree to which Jesus in obedience identifies with God. The other problem with this aspect of Hebblethwaite's construction of the necessity for full incarnational belief is that it is difficult to see in what sense God suffers in Jesus. Moltmann's idea[160] that God suffers in sending and abandoning his beloved Son on the cross for our salvation, in the separation or distancing himself from Jesus for our sake, is susceptible to the same criticism from Ward: surely God suffers in the sufferings of all his beloved children who die unjustly. They too are 'abandoned' in their suffering – we may assume, because of the place of free will in God's universe. Why must he send Jesus as a sign of his solidarity in suffering with us? Does Jesus' suffering hurt God more than ours? However important modern theologians may think it is to drop the classic idea of God's impassibility, the concept of the suffering of God is extremely difficult. The patristic problem with patripassianism has not been answered. We shall have to return to this elsewhere.

Finally, a real problem with Hebblethwaite's list of what would be lost if we do not have an incarnational christology is that he seems to commit the ought/is fallacy familiar to philosophers of ethics. He argues that the logical problems of the God-man concept are not insuperable; God could (and therefore by implication should) have become man, therefore he did.

> If God might have become man, but did not, then the reduced claim [in liberal Christology] for what God has done in Christ fails to satisfy us.[161]

We might argue in reply that if a doctrine of incarnation is logically conceivable but not the most apparently consistent, economic and appropriate conclusion to draw from the evidence, then the enhanced claim in conservative Christianity for what God has done in Christ also fails to satisfy and is not the best answer.

II

Salvation

1

Preliminary Thoughts

I have argued already that a religious faith worth following has a soteriological power; that certainly Christianity claims such saving power; and that for Christians salvation is held to have been achieved in some way through Jesus. I have also argued that belief in the divine and human nature of Jesus arose because people believed and experienced themselves saved through Jesus, and that on reflection it appeared that the only way to explain how Jesus saved was to ascribe to him both full humanity and full divinity. We have noted that it is not easy to comprehend or make sense of this notion, but we are told by traditionalist theologians that we must accept the mystery, as without it we can make no sense of the saving power in Christianity. Thus: christology is largely an attempt to meet the demands of soteriology.

As Schillebeeckx says,

> The patristic and indeed the whole Christian tradition has always attempted to define the actual person of Jesus in terms of the purport of the salvation brought by him. Because the salvation is 'imparted by God', the one who brought it was himself called divine, and thence it was concluded that Jesus was a divine person.[1]

We must be careful not to push this point too far. It is also true that 'we cannot make of Christianity just what we fancy'.[2] 'Faith utterances [about Jesus] must have a basis in the history of Jesus.'[3]

I shall be taking account of liberation theology later, and its emphasis on the practical results of Christian belief; but we might note now that Jon Sobrino, for example, warns that christology and soteriology are not identical. I do not agree with Sobrino's point that 'christology cannot begin with soteriology',[4] since I have already played my hand and said that this is precisely how christology begins. But Sobrino's real point here is true enough. We cannot begin with human problems, then diagnose what we need to solve those problems, and then invent a Jesus or an interpretation of Jesus who provides that solution. In that case, as Sobrino says, 'Christ would become a symbol, a value cipher, to be filled with whatever set of interests one might wish'.[5] There must be some evidence that the historical Jesus of Nazareth provides the solution, and even that our knowledge of the life and teaching of the historical Jesus affects our perception of the needs and the solution, or there is really no point in choosing Christianity at all.

However, as we shall note later, the confidence of liberation theologians as to how much of the historical Jesus can be recovered is perhaps over-optimistic, and the degree of interpretation of the history of Jesus by liberation theologians in the light of their own perception of the needs and necessary solution is more marked than Sobrino allows. In due course we shall have to examine the problem of a prior commitment to an ideology in much liberation theology.

Granting for the moment, however, that there is a connection between the work of the historical Jesus and the salvation for which we long, liberation theology arose because Latin American Christians were discovering that traditional Christian teaching about the person and work of Jesus was not helping them find salvation from the sociological circumstances of oppression and bondage.

European theologians like Moltmann and Metz had already begun to make a similar point. Christianity, like any religion, faces changing circumstances and changing needs. What constituted salvation for Jewish Christians or Reformation Christians was, perhaps, freedom from the consequences of religious or ritual law. Other Christians, living in fear of the power of hostile external enemies – devils, evil spirits, pagan emperors – might look for victory over these forces. But this might no longer constitute the kind of salvation needed by people oppressed under colonialism, or oppressed by the impersonality and loneliness of life in an urban jungle, or by the loss of clear purpose and ethical guidelines in a new and confusing age, or by powerlessness in the face of little-understood forces of world economy.